FRONTIERSMEN CAMPING FRATERNITY HANDBOOK

by JOHNNIE BARNES

GOSPEL PUBLISHING HOUSE
SPRINGFIELD, MISSOURI 65802

02-0706

DEDICATION

Sometimes in life our paths will cross and our lives will mingle with certain unique individuals whose spirit and dedication will leave our lives enriched.

Such a man was the late Elton Bell! He epitomized the spirit of FCF in all areas of his life. He was a true and loyal friend. His achievements in Royal Rangers and FCF are too numerous to mention. His courage was remarkable and his leadership was an inspiration to all. He led the way by being one of the first to complete the LTC, one of the first NTC staff members, one of the first FCF staff members, one of the first to achieve wilderness status, one of the first territorial representatives, and one of the first national vice-presidents. His skill as an outstanding outdoorsman will long be remembered.

We therefore dedicate this book to his memory. Although he has passed on to a higher and greater frontier, sometimes when we sit around a blazing FCF fire we sense his influence still among us.

JOHNNIE BARNES

ACKNOWLEDGMENTS

Special thanks to the following:

TO Fred Deaver for the section titled "The American Frontiersman" and the story "Heap of Trouble" and for the cover art and several other illustrations.

TO Dave Howard for the section titled "Frontier Clothing."

TO Jim Keefe for the article titled "The Care and Feeding of Muzzle Loaders."

TO Paul Johnson for the section titled "Frontier Foods."

TO David Barnes for layout and art.

CONTENTS

FRED
DEAVER

THE AMERICAN FRONTIERSMAN

Our history is full of men who contributed to the development of our nation.

A special breed of man in the long list of our country's forefathers was the old frontiersman. He was among the most colorful characters in American history, and yet he played a vital role in widening the borders of our land. He tamed virgin territory, making it safer for those who followed.

This rugged pioneer, like the modern astronaut, depended on his life-support equipment as he left the last settlement to explore the unknown. Let's look to those bygone days and see what equipment he used.

The frontiersman was usually clad in buckskin clothing. This garb was ideal for wilderness living. It was readily available and fairly easy to make. It was windproof, repelled the rain, was virtually snag proof, and took years to wear out.

He usually wore leather moccasins, which he replaced quite often.

Headgear was a coonskin cap, a wide-brimmed hat, a tricorn hat, or whatever headgear suited his fancy.

He carried a good rifle. It had two functions. First, it was for protection, and second and most important, it was used to supply food and clothing.

Along with the rifle, the frontiersman carried a rifle case made of buckskin.

In a hunting bag he carried a pouch containing rifle balls, extra flints, a small horn full of salt, a powder measure, a ball starter, and a roll of pillow ticking for patches.

He may have carried a few extra parts to repair his rifle, just in case it broke down. Probably he also carried a main spring, a screw or two, a tool kit, and maybe a screw driver or a pick to clean the flash hole.

On a strap of his hunting bag, he kept a small sharp knife, called a patch cutter.

If he had a flintlock, he usually carried two powder horns: a small one full of 4-F flash powder, and a large one that would hold 1 or 1½ pounds of 2- or 3-F powder.

On his belt he carried a knife, more than likely a butcher knife. Also slipped on the back of the belt was a good tomahawk.

Tucked over the belt in the front was often another pouch. In it he carried flint and steel for fire starting, along with a container of tinder to catch a spark to make a fire.

He may have had some jerky, pemmican, or parched corn to snack on. Any other personal items he needed he carried in this pouch.

If he had a packhorse, he carried many extra things to make his life in the unknown wilderness much easier.

Many adventuresome men who left for the wilderness in the early days of this country never made it back. Only those who took care of their equipment and knew how to use it had any chance of survival. There is an old saying that still holds true today: "Take care of your equipment, and it will take care of you."

The more I learn about these great American frontiersmen, the more I learn to appreciate them.

Appreciation for these colorful Americans was one of the reasons the national Royal Rangers Office selected the frontier theme as a basis for the Frontiersmen Camping Fraternity.

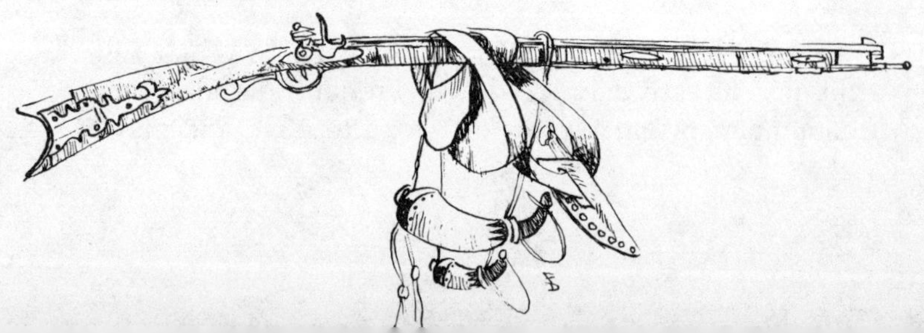

HISTORY OF FCF

The Frontiersmen Camping Fraternity was founded during the summer of 1966. For some time prior to this date, the national commander had felt the need for a special honor society to give recognition to men and older boys who had distinguished themselves in advancement, training, and camping.

The early American frontiersman was an excellent example of man's ability to adapt to the outdoors and the wilderness. His achievements were also an example of courage and determination. The national office, therefore, made the decision to base this fraternity on the lore and traditions of these early frontiersmen.

The first FCF chapter was organized in the Southern California District on July 8, 1966. High in the San Bernardino Mountains in a clearing surrounded by gigantic trees, a large group of Royal Rangers sat around a blazing campfire. As they waited, a feeling of mystery and expectancy filled the air.

Suddenly, the blast of a hunter's horn shattered the night's stillness and echoed through the trees. National Commander Johnnie Barnes stepped into the firelight, dressed in a buckskin outfit and a coonskin cap. As he began to explain the new FCF program, a hum of excitement rose above the sound of the crackling campfire. Assisted by two district leaders, Ron Halvorson and Bob Reid, these men proceeded with the first FCF callout. After pledging to endure a time of testing, the candidates were led away carrying a large rope to a mountaintop nearby for an all-night initiation.

Later as the new members (five men and five boys) were officially inducted into the fraternity at the final friendship fire, they sensed that this ceremony was a milestone in Royal Rangers history.

That same year, three more chapters were organized in the Northern California, the Southern Missouri, and the Iowa Districts. This exciting and unique fraternity has so captured the imaginations of men and boys until the program has now grown to include organized chapters in the majority of our districts.

PURPOSE OF FCF

1. To give recognition to men and boys who have shown exceptional interest and outstanding achievment in the Royal Rangers program and in Royal Rangers campcraft.

2. To build a brotherhood of "top-notch" men and boys over the years who will continue to be Royal Rangers program and camping enthusiasts.

3. To emphasize the importance of involvement in the advancement program, development of campcraft skills, and completion of the leadership-training programs.

4. To develop a corps of elite Royal Rangers who will strive to be the very best in Christian example and leadership.

BASIC REQUIREMENTS FOR MEMBERSHIP

BOYS

1. They must meet the following requirements:
   a. Earn the Trailblazer First Class rating.
   b. Earn the Advanced Camping Award.

2. They must be recommended by their outpost for this position. (This is done by submitting an FCF application form to the district office prior to the pow wow.)

3. After being selected, they must pass Phase I testing.
4. They will be officially "called out" by the FCF staff at a district pow wow during a council fire service.
5. They must participate in an initiation ceremony.

LEADERS

1. They must complete the leadership-training course and earn the Leader's Medal of Achievement.
2. They must be approved and selected by the FCF staff.
3. After being selected, they must pass Phase I.
4. They must participate in an initiation ceremony.

Requirements for additional steps of recognition, see page 43.

THE SPIRIT OF THE FRONTIERSMEN CAMPING FRATERNITY

The Frontiersmen Camping Fraternity endeavors to develop in each member the same courageous and undaunted spirit of the early frontiersmen. High morale and contagious enthusiasm are developed by urging each member to strive to achieve five important things. These five vital goals are to demonstrate courage, display achievement, develop friendships, demonstrate leadership, and develop woodsmanship.

DEMONSTRATE COURAGE

Early frontiersmen demonstrated outstanding courage by exploring unknown wilderness, scaling high mountains, crossing barren deserts, blazing trails in virgin forests, and by enduring extreme heat, cold, peril, and hardships. Many are the stories of their bravery in battle, their struggle for survival, and their unwavering loyalty in the name of honor. The Frontiersmen Camping Fraternity encourages each member to develop this same spirit of courage.

First, he must demonstrate courage by enduring a night of rugged initiation before he can qualify as a member. Many of the tests and ceremonies of this initiation demand a courageous spirit. Each frontiersman must continue to demonstrate a spirit of courage by taking an unwavering stand for the principles of Christianity, by squarely facing each personal problem, by bravely enduring each difficulty in life, and by promptly aiding those who need help, even at the risk of his own safety.

DISPLAY ACHIEVEMENT

History books are full of the accounts of such outstanding men as Lewis and Clark, Daniel Boone, Davey Crockett, and Kit Carson. These men along with many others carved a name for themselves in our American history because of their outstanding achievements. Their undaunted spirit of determination and their desire to excel provide some of the most colorful and exciting pages in our history books.

Frontiersmen Camping Fraternity members should also maintain this desire to excel and achieve. Proficiency in camping and other phases of the Royal Rangers program is demonstrated by achieving certain milestones in advancement. These abilities are further demonstrated by achieving certain milestones in addemonstrated by each candidate during his Phase I testing.

The Frontiersmen Camping Fraternity member should also strive to achieve the following goals: progress even further in advancement, become more involved in Royal Rangers, and continue to develop his skills as a good camper.

DEVELOP FRIENDSHIP

The saga of the American frontier contains many accounts of frontiersmen who gave or risked their lives and their fortunes on behalf of friends. Their unwavering loyalty to friends serves as an inspiration to today's frontiersmen. They too endeavor to cultivate the same strong bonds of friendship and display the same loyalty to their friends. This feeling of brotherhood is very strong in the Frontiersmen Camping Fraternity and every member does his best to uphold this tradition.

DEMONSTRATE LEADERSHIP

Many of today's major highways were once only blazed trails through uncharted wilderness, begun by an early frontiersman who led the way. Many of the routes through rugged mountain passes still used today were discovered by frontiersmen exploring new country.

Each FCF member should also be willing to step out and lead the way by being an example in Christian living, participating in Christian service, and by being willing to assume specific responsibilities. There are still many opportunities awaiting the individual who is willing and ready. So prepare yourself now for leadership so you'll be ready when the opportunity presents itself.

DEVELOP WOODMANSHIP

Early frontiersmen were able to adapt to almost any wilderness situation because they were constantly developing outdoor skills. It became a matter of survival to know what to do and how to do it. As experienced woodsmen, they could spend months on the frontier with only a small knapsack, a blanket, their rifle, and their hunting knife. Today's frontiersmen should also continue to develop outdoor skills. They should use every opportunity available to demonstrate these skills in a camping situation. A frontiersman should not only be a trained woodsman, but also an experienced woodsman.

FCF SYMBOL

The blazing campfire is the official symbol of the Frontiersmen Camping Fraternity. The campfire provided the early frontiersman with light and warmth and was essential for cooking. It was used for other vital needs as well.

The blazing campfire, therefore, symbolizes the spirit of FCF, which is PERSONAL WITNESSING (light), CHRISTIAN LOVE (warmth), and DEDICATED SERVICE (usefulness). There are five logs around the fire. These represent the five things needed to keep the spirit of FCF alive. They are COURAGE, ACHIEVEMENT, FRIENDSHIP, LEADERSHIP, and WOODSMANSHIP.

love
witness
dedication
COURAGE
ACHIEVEMENT
FRIENDSHIP
LEADERSHIP
WOODSMANSHIP

FCF Symbol

TRADITIONS

Even though this camping fraternity has a modern beginning, it has many traditions and ceremonies.

IDENTIFICATION STAFF

These personal staffs were driven into the ground by early frontiersmen and Indians during hunts to identify slain animals such as buffalo and deer. They were also placed in front of cabins and lodges to identify the owner.

In the Frontiersmen Camping Fraternity, these staffs are carried by members during Frontiersmen Camping Fraternity activities, placed in front of their shelters during outings and powwows, and driven into the ground in front of the member during Frontiersmen Camping Fraternity campfire ceremonies. These unique staffs have become a very colorful addition to Frontiersmen Camping Fraternity ceremonies and activities. The staffs are about 3 feet long and pointed to stick into the ground. Each member creates his own design by carving, painting, or attaching feathers, beads, etc. (See pages 19 and 20 for ideas.)

STALKING STICKS

During the Frontiersmen Camping Fraternity initiation each candidate receives a stalking stick. After the initiation, the new members may carve and burn these sticks into various shapes and designs. Next they are painted or varnished and then attached to a leather thong forming an Indian-type necklace. (The leather thongs are sometimes decorated with Indian beads.) These stalking sticks may be worn with the Frontiersmen Camping Fraternity outfits or simply kept by the members as a memento of their night of initiation.

IDENTIFICATION STAFFS

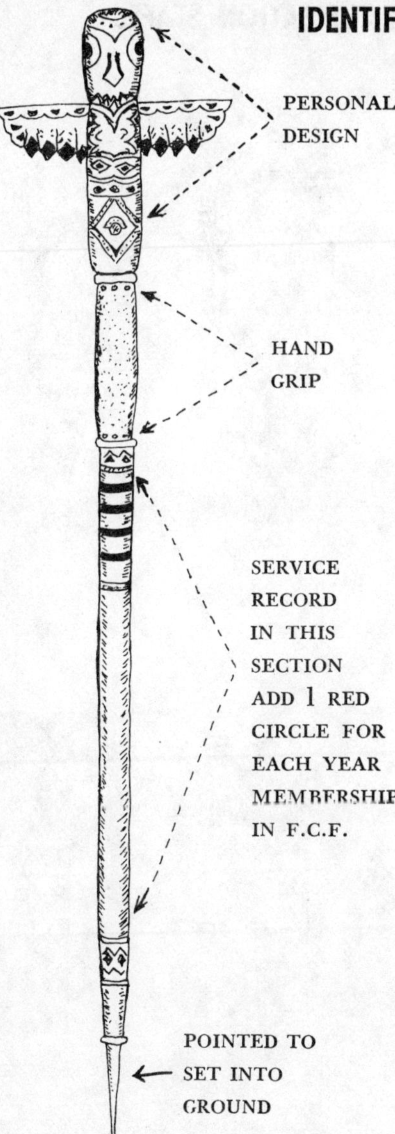

The staff should be about three feet long, and pointed to set into the ground. Create your own design by carving, painting, and using such materials as leather, buckskin, feather, brass tacks, beads, cloth, etc.

(Try to be original)

EXAMPLES OF IDENTIFICATION STAFFS

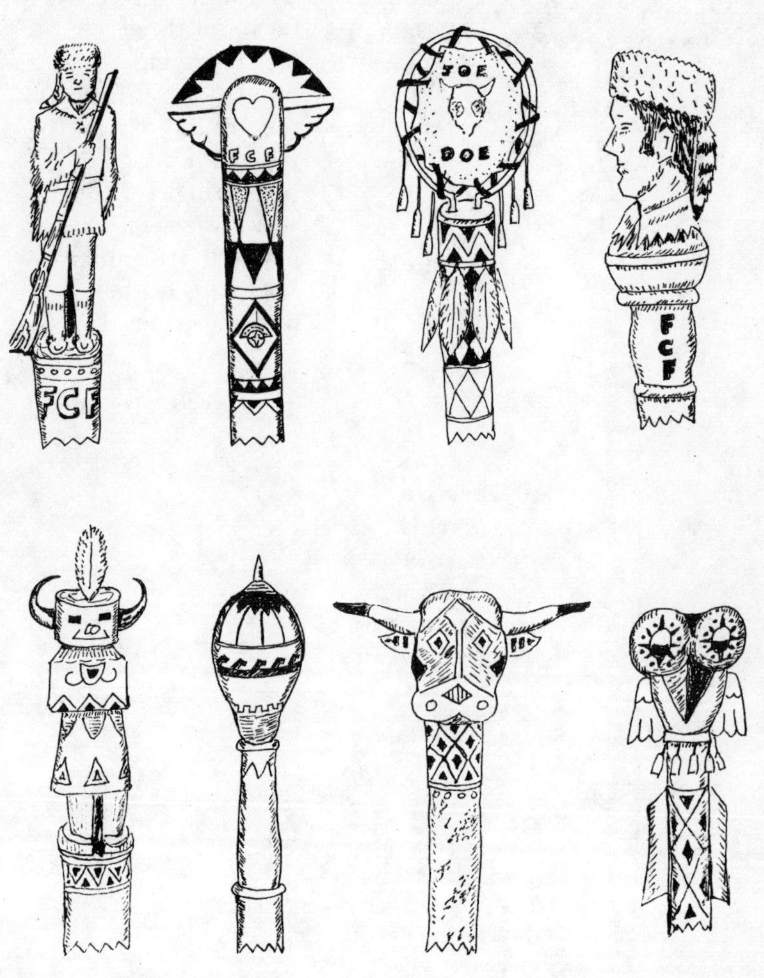

EXAMPLES OF STALKING STICK NECKLACES

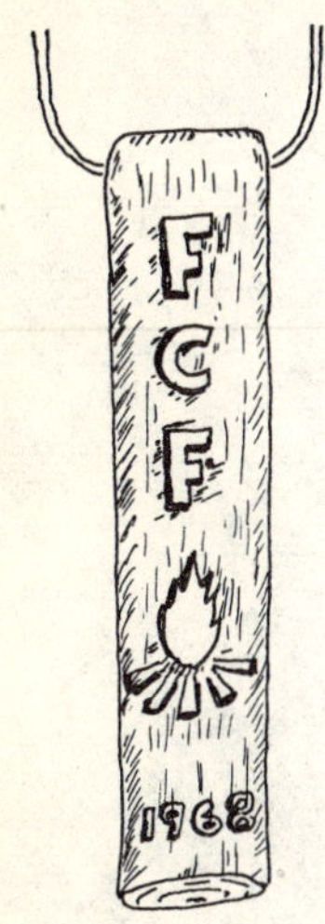

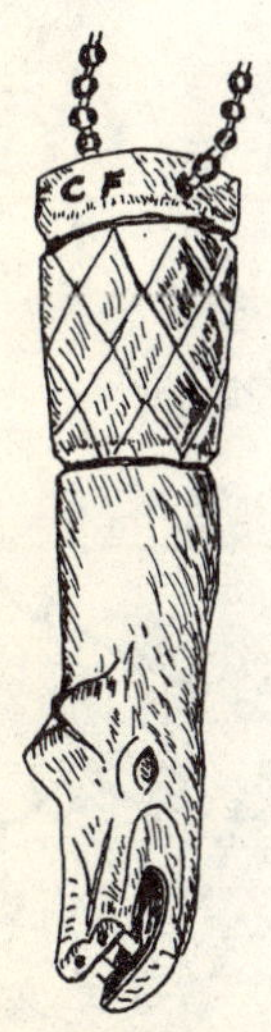

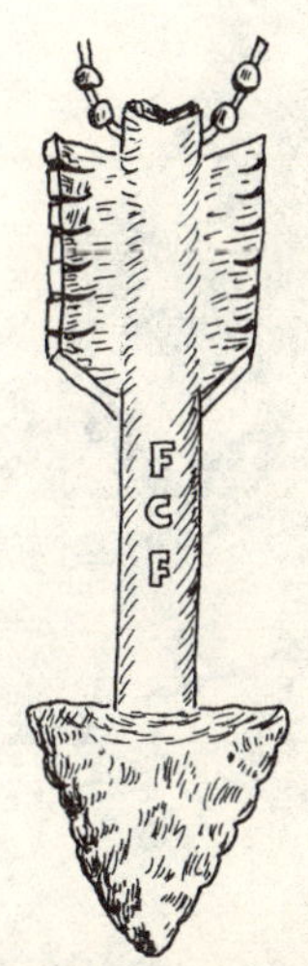

FRED SEAVER
1984

FRONTIERSMAN CLOTHING

HEADGEAR

There was a variety of headwear on the frontier, from the headdress used by the Indians to the store-bought felt or beaver hat. Many hats were made out of furs that the frontiersmen acquired. Fur from animals such as the skunk, raccoon, fox, coyote, cougar, deer, or bear was used by the frontiersmen.

Most of these selfmade hats were crude in nature and showed the individual's taste. Several had leather visors or bills on them. Some were made out of wamus (a strong, rough cloth), wool, or linen with fur added to them. Others were made from just leather.

Then there was the store-bought hat made from felt or beaver. These hats generally had a low crown and a wide brim.

Many a frontiersman, after selling all his hides in the spring, went on a buying fling. He sometimes bought city man's clothes, such as a white shirt with a stiff collar, a black suit with long split tails, or a stovepipe top hat or derby. When he headed back home to the frontier, it wasn't uncommon to see a mountainman still wearing his top hat even though he was back in his skins.

Hats were shaped and decorated to the individual's taste, with feathers and hatbands. Some of these hats were the round hat, tricorn hat, flop hat, Canadian cap, top hat, derby, fur hat, coonskin cap, leather hat, and beaver hat. Many of the mountainmen wore beaver hats in honor of the animals that provided them with their most valuable trading furs.

HATS

A. PLAINSMAN HAT
B. TRICORN HAT
C. FUR CAP

D. TOP HAT
E. ROUND HAT
F. VOYAGER FUR CAP

SHIRTS

The shirts worn by the frontiersmen varied from region to region. The materials were made from buckskin, elkskin, buffalo, calico, linen, wool, wamus (a strong, rough cloth), and cotton duck.

Jedidiah Smith (a famous frontiersman) usually bought each of his men 2 or 3 yards of calico so they could make their own shirts.

A frontiersman was not away from civilization for long before he wore out the clothing he brought from home. He then had to make his clothing from whatever he could find. Generally he used buckskin. Most of these shirts had fringe on them. The fringe was much longer than commonly believed. It helped to drain off the rain, and was a ready source of binding thongs.

Many shirts were decorated with beadwork, painted designs, and other items. Some different types of shirts found on the frontier were: French shirt, colonial shirt, waistcoat (somewhat like a vest), calico shirt, rifle frock, Plains Indian shirt, and trapper's shirt.

CALICO SHIRT

A. LEATHER COAT
B. COLONIAL SHOOTING FROCK
C. WAISTCOAT
D. COLONIAL SHIRT

A. INDIAN STYLE SHIRT
B. BUCKSKIN SHIRT
C. CAPOTE

COATS

Coats and robes were also a must during cold weather. Some of these coats were brought from home, but most were made on the frontier. Some coats did not have sleeves in them, but only protected the body. They were made from a variety of materials, such as buckskin, elkskin, buffalo, bear, wool, wamus, cotton duck, and blankets. Some of these coats still had the fur on them and were worn with the fur inside for warmth, and the hide outside for rain protection. A coat made out of a blanket was called a capote. These generally were made from a 4-point Hudson Bay blanket. Knee-length coats made from cloth were called cassocks.

In addition to coats, there were robes. These robes were made from larger animals such as buffalo, elk, bear, and moose. Usually these robes still had the hair on them and were wrapped around the individual for warmth. They were also used as blankets.

Sometimes a cape or yoke was worn during cool weather. This was a piece of buckskin worn just over the shoulders.

PANTS AND LEGGINGS

Pants on the frontier were simple and plain. It was not until late in the days of the frontier that pockets were added to pants.

The materials used for pants were usually linen, wamus (a strong, rough cloth), cotton duck, and leather. Types of pants were: overalls (not like today's overalls), trousers, mountainman pants, and buffalo-hunter pants.

A. BUCKSKIN PANTS

B. LEGGINGS
C. BREECH CLOTH
D. COLONIAL SHORT BREECHES

On the eastern frontier one might see knee-length breeches, which were made out of cloth. Some pants were decorated with beadwork.

Leggings were two separate pants legs, without a midsection. Leggings were held up by a leather strap tied to a sash or belt. Breech cloths were worn with leggings to give protection to the midsection. They were tucked under the sash or belt in the back and front. Breech cloths were made from a variety of materials. Leggings are not to be confused with gaiters.

FOOTWEAR

The moccasin was the chief footwear on the frontier. Moccasins were made from different kinds of leather. Some were decorated ornately while others were plain. When moccasins wore out, instead of throwing them away, the frontiersman would often make a new pair and wear them on top of the old pair. The Indians made moccasins for the left and right feet, while the cobbler made boots or shoes to fit either foot.

Square-toed shoes with large buckles were common on the eastern frontier. Also boots with square toes or rounded toes were often seen on the eastern and western frontiers. However, once these boots or shoes wore out, the frontiersman had to change to moccasins.

Gaiters were also related to footwear. Gaiters were made of leather, wamus, or cotton duck. The gaiter was for added protection to the lower leg and ankle. They were worn over the pants from the knee down and covered the instep.

FOOTWEAR

A. MOCCASIN
B. FRINGED MOCCASIN BOOT
C. SADDLE BOOT
D. COLONIAL BUCKLE SHOE

HOW TO MAKE A FRONTIERSMAN SHIRT

Rip apart an old shirt and use it as a pattern. The front and back are alike except an opening is cut in the front. This front opening is held together with a leather string. Make front and back slightly longer than a regular shirt. Leave a 3-inch slit on each side at the bottom of the shirt. Additional strips of leather fringe are added to the front, back, and sleeves of the shirt. Attach the collar after the front and back are joined together.

Shirts may also be made without a collar, or they may be split all the way down the front and worn like a coat.

A leather thong may be used to close the front of the shirt if desired. Try to make the shirt look authentic. Patterns for shirt and other clothing may be purchased from a number of black powder stores.

PATTERN FOR FRONTIERSMAN SHIRT

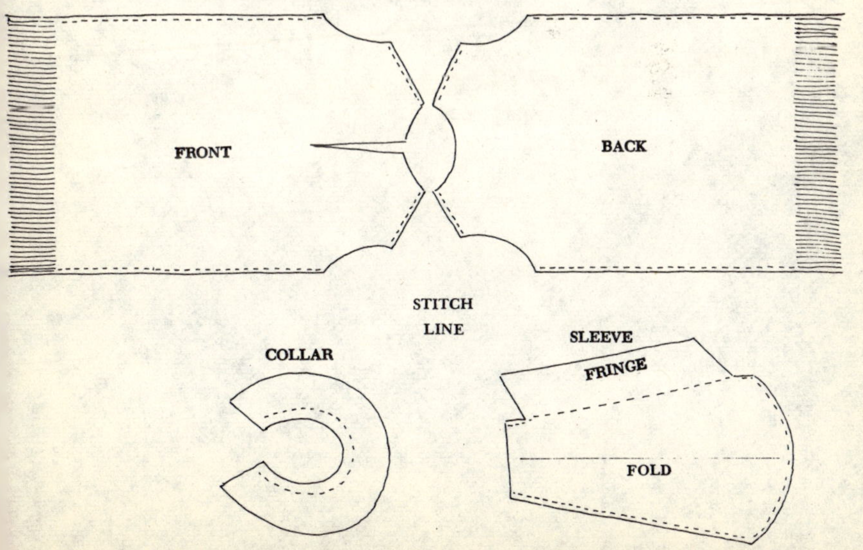

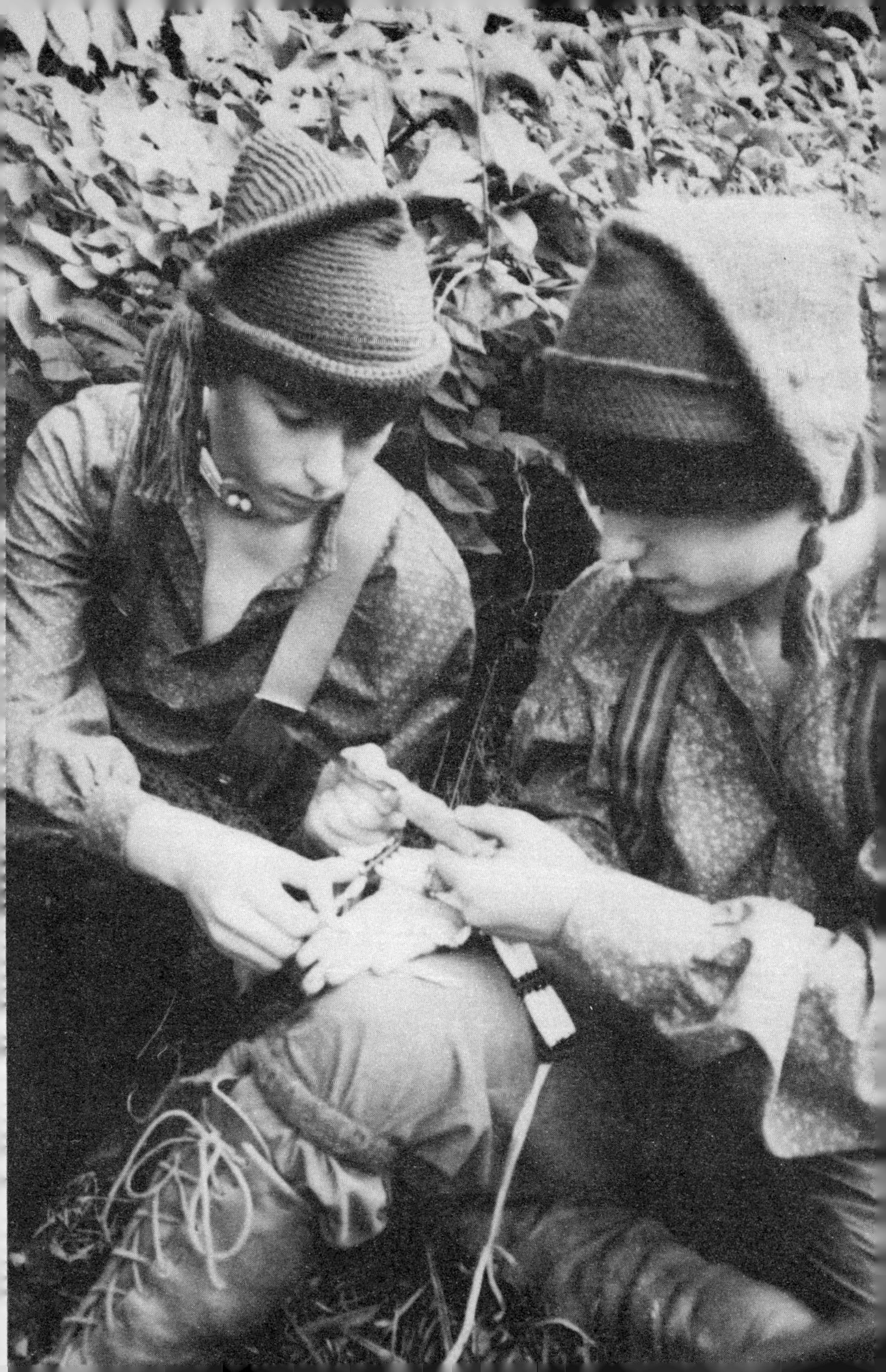

SOME DOS AND DON'TS

1. No patches such as Royal Rangers pow wow patches, district FCF patches, or any other patch of this nature should be on an FCF costume. These were not a part of the frontier costume.

2. No tooled leatherwork on belts or other items.

3. No eagle claws or feathers. It is illegal to possess any part of an eagle unless it is registered with the federal government.

4. No owl or hawk feathers or claws. It is illegal to possess any part of an owl or a hawk. They are protected by the federal government.

5. Bear claws are not to be bought or sold unless state regulations permit it.

6. Buttons should be made from horn, wood, leather, shell (not metallic cartridges), pewter, or brass. Some coins during frontier times were made into buttons.

7. If possible, no zippers or plastic buttons. They are not in keeping with frontier character.

ACCESSORIES

The following is a list of some of the accessories a frontiersman may have worn or used. It is not necessary to secure them all. However, you may wish to make or secure some of them to give your outfit that completely authentic look.

RIFLES

There were two types of muzzle-loading rifles used by the frontiersmen: the flintlock and the percussion rifle. The flintlock rifle utilized the flint and frizzen to ignite the powder in the pan, which in turn exploded the powder in the barrel. The percussion rifle used a percussion cap on a percussion nipple to ignite the barrel.

There were two general styles of rifles used by the frontiersmen. They were the Long rifle and the Hawkins rifle. The Kentucky Long rifle (which was actually made in Pennsylvania), was the most commonly used east of the Mississippi. However, as the frontiersman moved westward, he needed a shorter gun to carry in the saddle. Also, he encountered larger game, such as the grizzly bear and the buffalo, which required a larger caliber rifle.

In the early 1800's, a man named Jacob Hawkins developed a shorter .50-caliber rifle that became very popular with the frontiersmen. All rifles of this style soon began to be called "Hawkins" rifles.

Many reproductions of these different types and styles of rifles may be purchased today. However, be cautious when buying a rifle and make sure you secure a good, reliable weapon. Inferior reproductions can be dangerous.

Never attempt to give a demonstration on the use of a muzzle-loading rifle or enter into a black-powder shoot without first learning how to properly load, shoot, and care for your rifle—under the supervision of a reliable instructor. Black-powder rifles are just as dangerous as any other firearm. Never treat them like a toy. Secure an FCF shooters card.

RIFLES

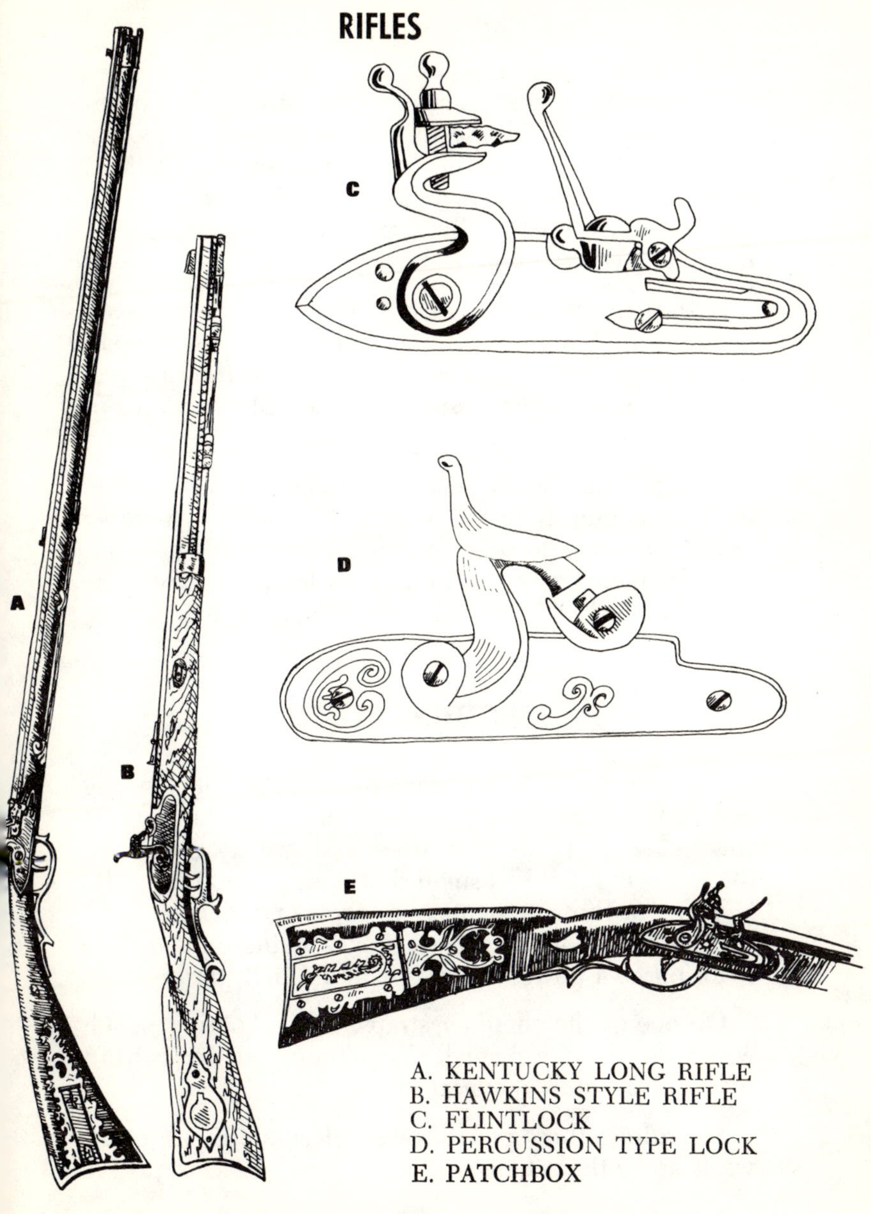

A. KENTUCKY LONG RIFLE
B. HAWKINS STYLE RIFLE
C. FLINTLOCK
D. PERCUSSION TYPE LOCK
E. PATCHBOX

POWDER HORN

Powder horns were usually made from cow horns. Most frontiersmen made their own powder horns, and carved and engraved them to suit their fancy. Most horns were shaved down thin enough so they could hold the horn up to a light and be able to determine how much powder was in the horn.

If the frontiersman had a flintlock, he needed two horns: a small horn containing fine powder for the pan, and a larger horn with coarser powder for the rifle barrel. If he used a percussion rifle, he only needed one powder horn.

Commercially made powder horns may be purchased from many gun shops today. However, an FCF member will treasure his powder horn much more if he makes it himself. If he carves and engraves his horn, it will be even more valuable.

SHOOTING POUCH

The shooting pouch, sometimes called a hunting pouch, was used to carry items used while shooting. It was generally made of leather and usually contained the following items: a small shot pouch containing rifle balls, extra flints or percussion caps, material for making patches, tools for cleaning or working on the rifle, spare parts, a powder measure, and a ball starter.

On one of the shoulder straps of his shooting pouch was a sheath with a small sharp knife used for cutting off surplus patch material.

Sometimes these pouches were decorated with beadwork and other items.

RIFLE ACCESSORIES

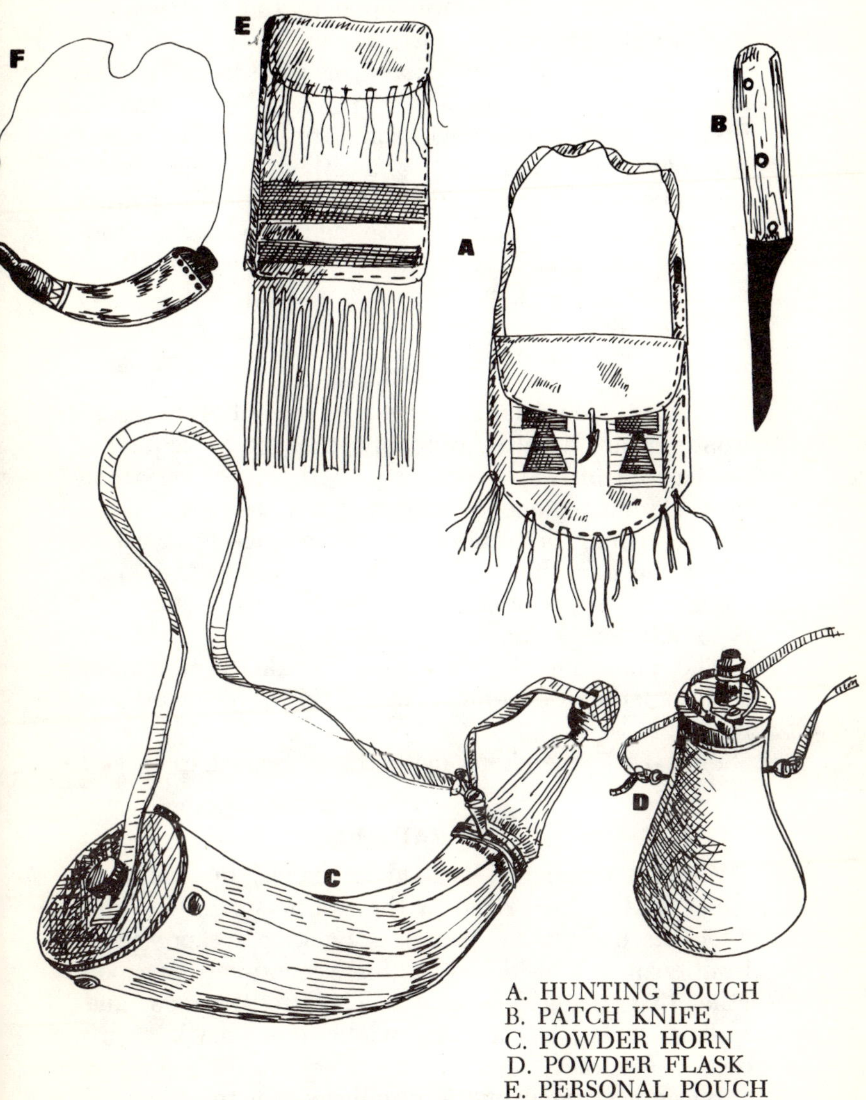

A. HUNTING POUCH
B. PATCH KNIFE
C. POWDER HORN
D. POWDER FLASK
E. PERSONAL POUCH
F. SALT HORN

PERSONAL POUCH

In addition to a shooting pouch, the frontiersman sometimes carried a personal pouch. Because his trousers had no pockets, this pouch was used to carry items normally carried in pockets. It probably contained his firebox (flint and steel), some tinder, some jerky, pemmican, parched corn, and other personal items. These pouches were usually made from pliable leather or skins. Sometimes they were decorated with beadwork or paintings depicting his personal totem. Hand-making this pouch is an excellent project for every FCF member.

KNIFE

A good, dependable knife was essential to every frontiersman. It was probably the most frequently used of all his hand tools. He used it for everything from skinning game to trimming his toenails. It was used by many a frontiersman as a back-up weapon when the one shot in his rifle was used. The knife came in a variety of styles, but usually was a standard-type skinning knife.

The knife sheath was usually made from leather and sometimes decorated with fringe, beadwork, or brass brads.

Some FCF members make their own knives and sheaths.

TOMAHAWK

A good tomahawk (called a "hawk" by frontiersmen), was highly prized by the frontiersman. He wore it on the back of his belt as a back-up weapon. The frontiersman considered it his second-best weapon (the first being his rifle). The frontiersmen and Indians alike learned to wield the "hawk" with deadly accuracy.

Because a tomahawk is usually within the financial

HARDWARE

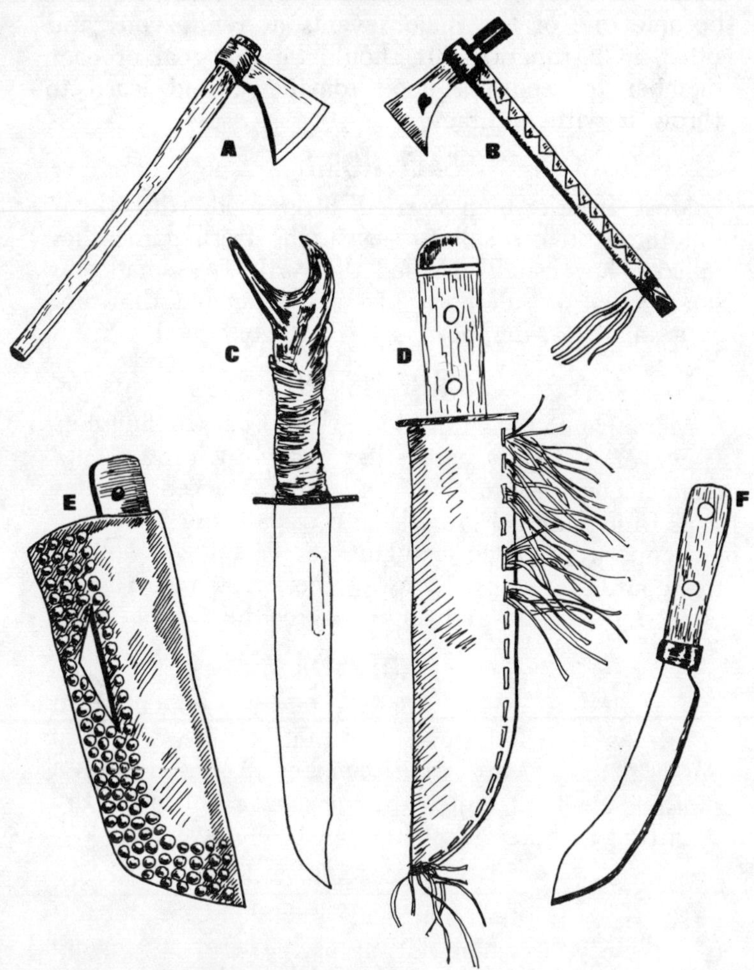

A. THROWING TOMAHAWK
B. INDIAN TRADING HAWK
C. HANDMADE BONE HANDLE KNIFE
D. SHEATH KNIFE WITH FRINGE SHEATH
E. GREEN RIVER SKINNING KNIFE WITH STUDDED
   SHEATH
F. PATCH KNIFE

range of every FCF member, "hawk throwing" has become one of the major events at rendezvous and other FCF functions. It should be the goal of each member to secure a good tomahawk and learn to throw it with accuracy.

SALT HORN

Most frontiersmen carried little food with them, but they did use salt to season the fresh game they killed. They usually carried their salt in a small cow horn called a "salt horn." It was somewhat the same as a small powder horn, except it contained salt.

DRINKING CUP

Many frontiersmen used a tin cup as a drinking cup. However, in many cases they made their own cups from a cow or buffalo horn. Others carved wooden cups from the burl growth on a tree. These hollowed-out cups were called "noggins." Some utilized hollow, dry gourds for cups. Many of the horns and wooden cups were carved and engraved by the frontiersmen.

TINDERBOX

A tinderbox was a small waterproof container in which was carried flint, steel, and charred cloth to build a fire. Every FCF member should secure a flint-and-steel set and learn the art of starting a fire with flint and steel—just like our forefathers did.

GUN CASE

The early frontiersmen made buckskin cases to protect their rifle when not in use. These cases were usually decorated with fringe and beadwork.

CAPPER

A capper was a device made from a heavy piece of leather that was punched with small holes to hold percussion caps for a percussion rifle.

ACCESSORIES

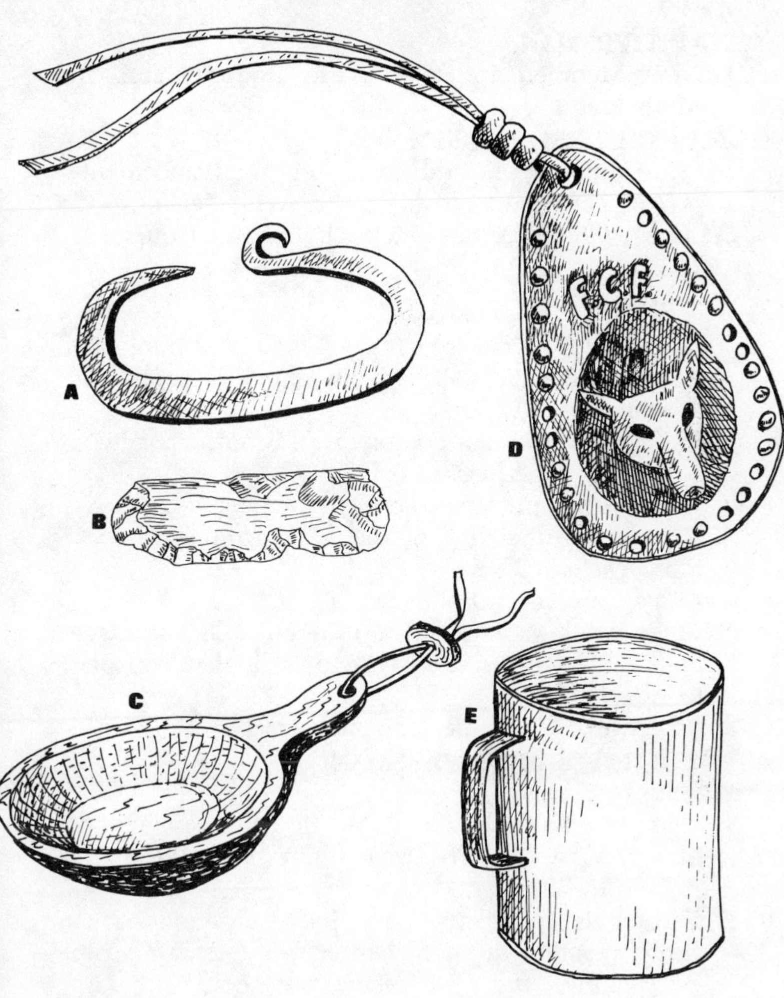

A. FLINT STRIKER
B. FLINT STONE
C. NOGGIN CUP

D. PERCUSSION CAPPER
E. TIN CUP

STEPS OF RECOGNITION IN F.C.F.

FRONTIERSMAN:
1. New Membership (see "Basic Requirements for Membership")

BUCKSKIN FRONTIERSMAN:
BOYS: Complete one additional step in advancement— or earn the Gold Medal of Achievement.

MEN: 1. Complete the new FCF Training Course.

2. Tutor a boy into FCF.

BOTH MEN AND BOYS:
1. Participate in at least one FCF initiation; and be an active member in your chapter for at least 1 year.
2. Make or purchase a complete FCF outfit and wear it at FCF functions.
3. Recite from memory the FCF pledge.
4. Explain the meaning of the FCF symbol.
5. State the purpose of FCF.
6. Make an FCF ID staff.
7. Make your stalking stick into an FCF necklace.
8. Select a frontier-related craft or skill that you plan to develop.
9. Select an FCF name for yourself.

WILDERNESS FRONTIERSMAN:
BOYS
1. Complete one additional step in advancement and earn the Survival Award or earn the Gold Medal of Achievement.
2. Participate in at least two initiations and be an active member in your chapter for at least 2 years.
3. Be sponsored by a Wilderness member.
4. Carry a wilderness pouch for at least 3 months.
5. Tutor another boy in FCF.
6. Pass a previgil testing session.
7. Complete an all-night vigil.

MEN

1. Attend and complete a National Training Camp.
2. Participate in at least four initiations and be an active member in your chapter for at least 2 years.
3. Be sponsored by your district chapter.
4. Carry a wilderness pouch for at least 3 months.
5. Tutor a boy into FCF.
6. Pass a previgil testing session.
7. Complete an all-night vigil.

APPROVAL AND SUPERVISION

Each step of recognition for a Buckskin must be approved by the chapter staff before the member is eligible to wear the recognition pin.

The all-night vigil and previgil test for Wilderness Frontiersmen must be conducted under the supervision of a regional coordinator, a territorial representative, or by a member of the national staff.

F.C.F. RECOGNITION PINS:

FRONTIERSMAN

BUCKSKIN FRONTIERSMAN

WILDERNESS FRONTIERSMAN

FRONTIER SKILLS

Many of the skills and crafts of our forefathers are fast disappearing from the American scene. One of the goals of FCF is to master and preserve these skills, and then pass them on to others. The following are some of the frontier skills an FCF member may develop.

BLACK POWDER SHOOTING

Learning how to load, shoot, and care for a muzzle-loading rifle is an intriguing skill to develop. These skills are best learned under the tutoring of a skilled instructor.

SAFETY RULES

There are rules you must observe if you plan to use a muzzle loader.

1. Know how to use your rifle properly before entering a shooting match or giving a demonstration to others.
2. Never use live ammunition when using your rifle in a skit.
3. Never keep a loaded firearm in camp.
4. Load your firearm at a firing line only.
5. All powder horns must be capped or closed before firing your rifle.
6. During a shooting match, obey the range officer promptly.
7. The muzzle of the rifle must be kept in the direction of the target or in the air until fired.
8. It is strongly recommended that you wear safety or shooting glasses for competition.
9. A safety shield must be worn when a flintlock is fired while standing side by side with another shooter.

10. A muzzle-loading rifle is a deadly weapon, treat it
    as such.

BLACK POWDER SHOOTERS CARD

As a safeguard against possible accidents by unqualified individuals, in Royal Rangers no one should be allowed to fire a muzzle-loading rifle during a council fire, as a demonstration, or on a firing range, unless he possesses a shooters card.

The individual must demonstrate, before an experienced black powder shooter, his ability to properly and safely load and fire a muzzle-loading rifle. He must also orally demonstrate his knowledge and understanding of the black powder safety rules listed in the *FCF Handbook*.

The qualifier is usually the FCF chapter president. If the chapter president does not have the expertise in black powder shooting, this responsibility may be assigned to a qualified, experienced black powder shooter.

All shooters cards should be signed by the chapter president. If another qualifier is used, both he and the president should sign the card.

The FCF chapter president will make sure that an opportunity is given each experienced shooter to qualify for the shooters card without long delay and that each card is promptly signed.

The following article by Jim Keefe, a Missouri conservation officer, should be helpful in learning more about a muzzle-loading rifle.

THE CARE AND FEEDING OF MUZZLE LOADERS

By Jim Keefe

One Christmas a young man received a muzzle-loader pistol kit as a present from his wife. He put in a number of hours assembling the thing, then started the rounds of sporting-goods stores to get powder and balls to shoot it. Like many people these days, it was his first contact with black-powder firearms and he knew nothing about shooting and caring for his pistol, beyond the scanty instructions that came with the kit.

Unfortunately, some sporting-goods dealers who sell these kits have no experience in handling such firearms either. This young man asked for some black powder and the dealer gave him a can of shotshell reloading powder. He thought it ought to do, because its color was certainly black.

On the 12th firing the pistol blew up in his hand. He was lucky, because other than a numbness in his hand and arm, he was not hurt, and neither were the three companions clustered around him.

Black powder is more than just black in color. It is the name of a particular kind of gun powder made expressly for muzzle-loading arms. No other kind of powder should be used in such arms. Modern smoke-less powders generate too much pressure for muzzle loaders.

With the advent a few years ago of renewed interest in the muzzle loaders, a great number of individuals have gone into the black-powder shooting sport without serving some apprenticeship in learning the dos and don'ts. There is no real substitute for learning how to handle and shoot black-powder arms under the guidance of an experienced shooter, but the following tips may help introduce the newcomer into the field, without some of the dangers he might otherwise run into. First, let's learn how to load a percussion rifle.

1. Make sure the barrel is clean and free of obstructions. You do this by measuring with the ramrod. Thrust the ramrod into the barrel as far as it will go and mark the spot where it emerges from the barrel. Place the ramrod along the outside of the barrel, marked spot at the muzzle. If it reaches down as far as the drum or bolster, the gun probably is not loaded. To check further, blow through it with the hammer on half-cock. You should have a free passage of air. If circumstances permit, snap a cap on it, with the muzzle pointed toward dust, a leaf blade, or grass. The grass or dust should move if the passage is clear.

2. Let the hammer down, if you haven't snapped a cap, to prevent some of the powder charge being blown out through it when seating the ball.

3. Set the rifle on its stock, barrel pointing up.

4. Using a powder measure, pour the recommended charge of black powder only into the barrel. Black powder marked Fffg is good for rifles up to and including .45 caliber; Ffg for larger bores.

5. Place a lubricated patch on top of the muzzle. The lubricant can be one of the commercial products sold for this purpose, Crisco, or, if the gun is to be shot at once, saliva. Patching material ordinarily will be pillow ticking, but choice of material depends on the fit of the ball to the individual gun. You'll have to experiment with this, but stick to plain cotton, not synthetic blends.

6. Place a ball of the proper caliber on the patch material.

7. Using your short starter, push the ball and patching material into the barrel, flush with the muzzle or slightly below.

8. Cut off the excess patch material with a sharp patch knife.

9. Push the ball and patch downward as far as your long starter will go.

10. Using your ramrod, push the ball down the barrel with a smooth motion and seat it firmly on the powder charge. This is important: no air must be left between the patched ball and the powder charge. Do not hammer or bounce the ramrod on the ball. It will deform it and affect accuracy.

11. Place the hammer at half-cock and put a percussion cap on the nipple. Your gun is now ready to fire.

To load a flintlock rifle, you must first place a sharp gunflint, sandwiched in a piece of soft leather, between the jaws of the cock (hammer), and tighten.

1. Be sure barrel and touchhole are clean and free of oil and obstruction. (Same as with a percussion arm.)

2. Place hammer at half-cock and lower frizzen onto the pan to prevent powder being blown out when seating the ball. Guns without half-cock position should not have frizzen lowered.

3. Follow steps 3 through 10 to load powder and patched ball.

4. Raise the frizzen and pour a small amount of priming powder into the pan. Black powder marked Ffffg is best, but you can make your own priming powder by grinding coarser powder in a saucer with a spoon or in a ceramic mortar with a pestle.

5. Lower frizzen, and your flintlock is now ready to fire.

To load a muzzle-loading shotgun, again make sure barrel or barrels are clean and free of oil and obstructions.

1. Pour a measured charge of Ffg black powder into the barrel. Recommended loads for medium power are:

   10 gauge—4¼ drams (115 grains) and 1½ oz. of shot.
   12 gauge—3½ drams (95 grains) and 1½ oz. of shot.
   16 gauge—3 drams (80 grains) and 1 oz. of shot.
   20 gauge—2½ drams (70 grains) and 1 oz. of shot.
   410 cal.—1½ drams (40 grains) and ½ oz. of shot.

2. Using your ramrod, push a wad down the barrel onto the powder charge and tamp it firmly. Commercially manufactured fiber wads or "power-piston"-type wads will work if they fit the bore well. A fiber wad should be at least ¾-inch thick. Wasp nest is sometimes used also.

3. Using a shot measure, pour the recommended amount of shot into the barrel.

4. With your ramrod, push an "overshot" wad on top of the shot. This is usually a thin cardboard that fits the barrel tightly with a friction fit. An inexpensive and effective wad can be a single sheet of toilet tissue wadded up and pushed firmly onto the shot. Crumpled wasp nest also serves.

5. Place a percussion cap on the nipple, or prime the pan, and you're ready to shoot.

Bullets used in muzzle loaders always should be pure lead, as soft as you can find. Scratching the lead with your thumbnail will tell you if it is suitable. Wheel-weight metal and linotype metal is too hard for muzzle loaders.

To clean your muzzle loader, use a commercial black-powder solvent or plain soap and water. I like to place a piece of leather over the nipple, under the hammer, and pour some solvent into the barrel and let it stand for a few minutes. A round toothpick in the touchhole of a flintlock will serve as a plug. Pour the solvent out and then wipe the bore with dry patches until they come clean. Be sure to wipe your lock, nipple, and barrel with cleaner, too.

Apply a good oil or water-displacing lubricant like WD-40 to the barrel, inside and out, and to the lock. Now and then, remove and thoroughly clean the inside of your lock and keep it well lubricated.

It's a good idea to use a nipple wrench and unscrew the nipples and clean the passage between nipple and barrel with pipe cleaners. A pipe cleaner is good for cleaning flintlock touchhole areas too.

Cleaning black-powder guns is important, as both black powder and percussion caps are extremely corrosive.

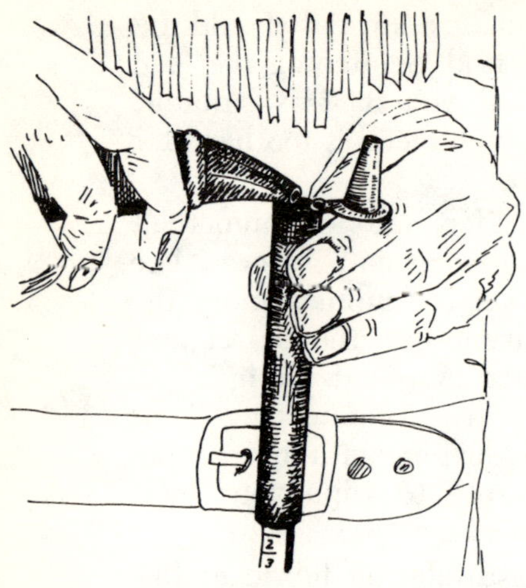

Measure the charge of black powder

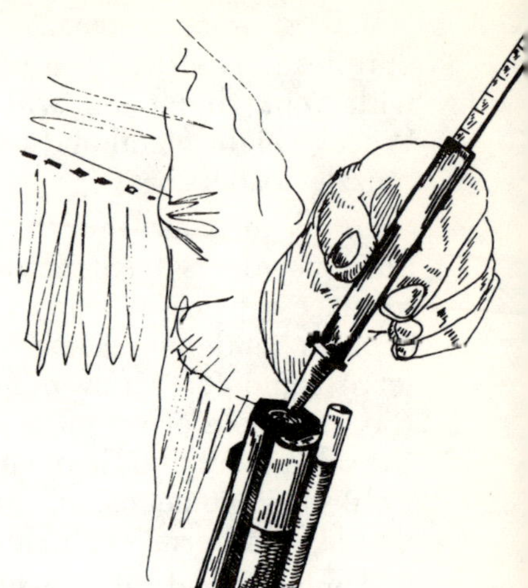

Pour powder into the clean barrel

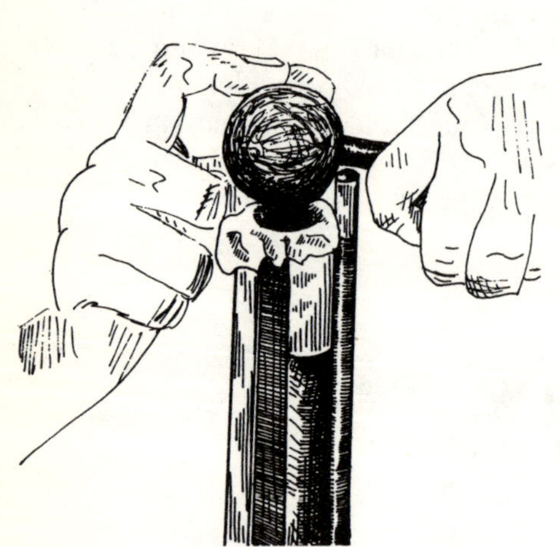

Press bullet and patch into muzzle

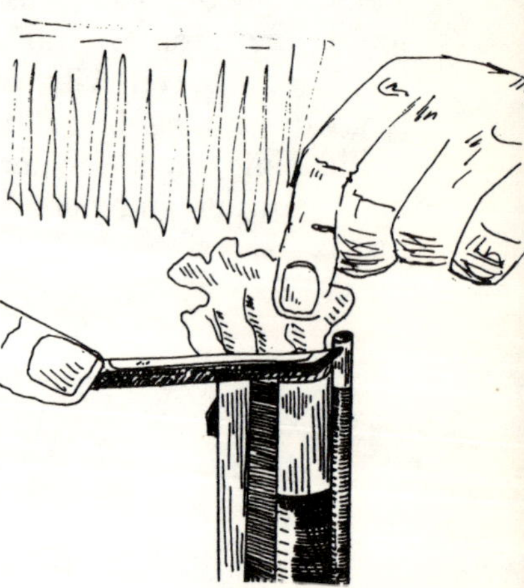

Trim excess patch with sharp knife

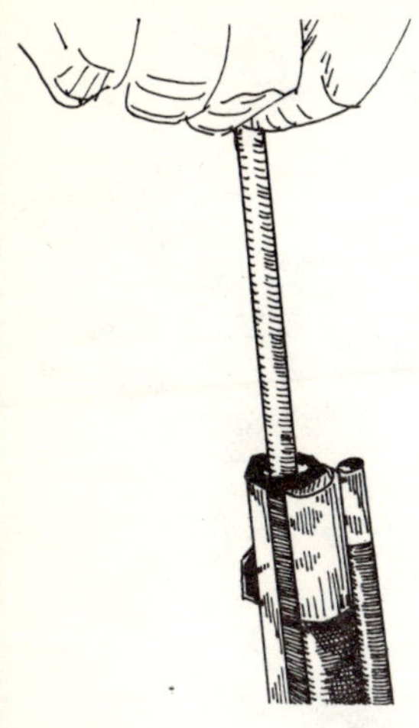

Starter gets bullet down barrel

Seat ball on powder with ramrod

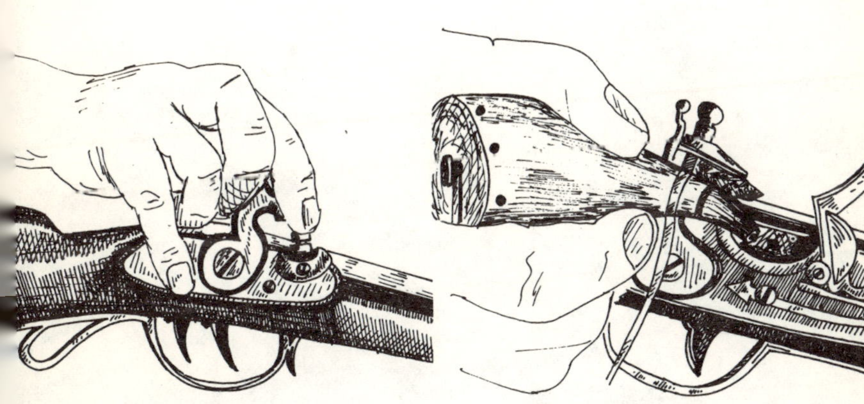

Place percussion cap on nipple

Charge flintlock pan with powder

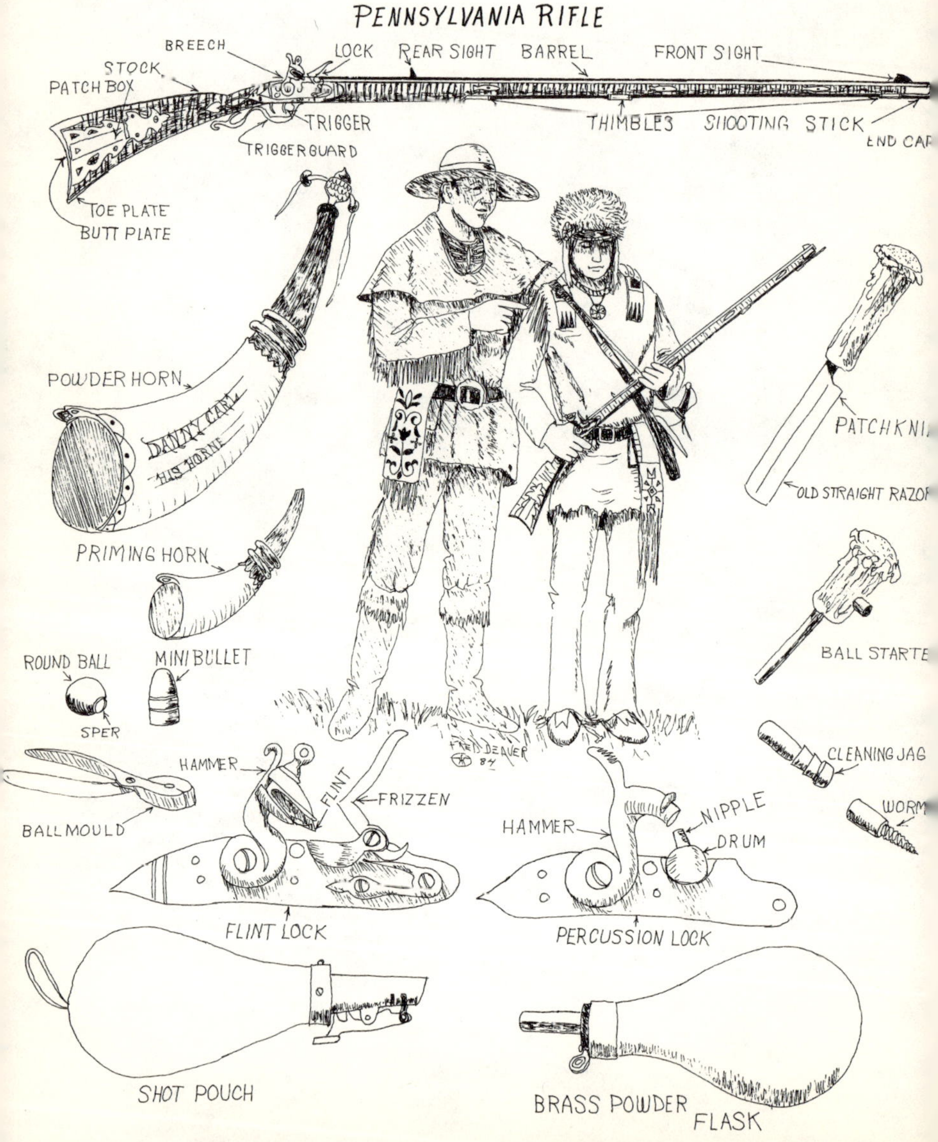
PENNSYLVANIA RIFLE
BREECH
LOCK
REAR SIGHT
BARREL
FRONT SIGHT
STOCK
PATCH BOX
TRIGGER
THIMBLES
SHOOTING STICK
END CAP
TRIGGERGUARD
TOE PLATE
BUTT PLATE
POWDER HORN
DANNY CARL
HIS HORNE
PATCHKNI
OLD STRAIGHT RAZOR
PRIMING HORN
BALL STARTE
ROUND BALL
MINI BULLET
SPER
FRED DEAVER
84
CLEANING JAG
HAMMER
FLINT
FRIZZEN
BALLMOULD
WORM
NIPPLE
HAMMER
DRUM
FLINT LOCK
PERCUSSION LOCK
SHOT POUCH
BRASS POWDER
FLASK

FLINT AND STEEL

Four items are needed to start a fire with flint and steel:

1. Charred cloth to catch the spark.
2. Flint or quartz.
3. Steel.
4. Tinder.

To start the fire, do the following:

1. Place tinder on the ground or a solid surface.
2. Place charred cloth on top of tinder.
3. Hold flint and steel firmly with your fingers.
4. Strike glancing blows vertically against edge of steel, showering spark into charred cloth. (Some prefer to strike with the steel; some prefer to strike with the flint.)
5. When a spark is caught in the charred cloth and begins to glow, place it in the tinder.
6. Lift tinder and blow briskly on the charred cloth until the flame starts.

To master this skill, the secret is good charred cloth, very dry tinder, and practice, practice, practice.

Charring Cloth for Flint and Steel

MATERIALS NEEDED:

Cotton cloth   Scissors
Old coffee can   Hot plate
Old shoe-polish can

1. Cut cotton cloth the same size as shoe-polish can.
2. Place 10 or 12 cloth discs in coffee can. Place can on hot plate. (Open fire may be used.)
3. Allow cloth to char until it is black. (Be sure to do this outside as there will be much SMOKE!)
4. Place charred discs in polish can for future use. (Can keeps discs dry.)

FRED DEAVER
1984

Tinder

A good tinder may be made from:

1. The inside of old bird nests.
2. The shredded bark of cedar.
3. The inner bark of dead cottonwood or basswood.
4. Fine wood scrapings.
5. Very dry dead weeds or grass.

PLEASE NOTE: Shape tinder into round wads before using.

TOMAHAWK THROWING

An exciting skill that every FCF member should develop is tomahawk throwing. The tomahawk is usually referred to as a "hawk" in the FCF program.

Before attempting this skill, secure a reliable tomahawk with a stout handle. Be sure the hawk head is secure on the handle before throwing. The secret is distance and form. A tomahawk must turn one complete revolution in the air before it will stick in the target. For the average-size person with the average-size hawk, six paces is about the right distance for one revolution.

After stepping off your paces, grip the hawk firmly by the end of the handle, with the hawk blade vertical with the target. Take one step forward, at the same time throwing the hawk in an overhead swing, much as you would throw a rock or baseball. Keep your swing smooth and your wrist straight. If the hawk does not hit on the blade, adjust your pace until you find the right distance. You may also need to adjust your swing so you neither throw too hard nor too lightly. Always observe basic safety rules when throwing the hawk.

With practice, you too can become proficient and accurate with the tomahawk.

KNIFE THROWING

Another interesting activity that requires a lot of skill is knife throwing. It is best to use a knife that is designed for throwing. It is very easy to break the blade of an ordinary thin-blade knife if you use it for throwing.

The secret of knife throwing is also distance and form. However, it is much more difficult to get the right pace and the right form for knife throwing than it is for tomahawk throwing.

The knife may be thrown either by the blade or by the handle. It is thrown in an overhead swing, much as you would throw a rock.

Each individual must establish the proper distance for his knife to do one revolution in the air before hitting the target. This varies with the length of a person's arm and the size of the knife. The individual must also use exactly the same form each time. Since the knife must hit on a very small point, it takes a great deal of precision to be accurate. This skill, therefore, will require much practice.

Knife throwing can be dangerous, so be sure to follow basic safety rules at all times when throwing a knife.

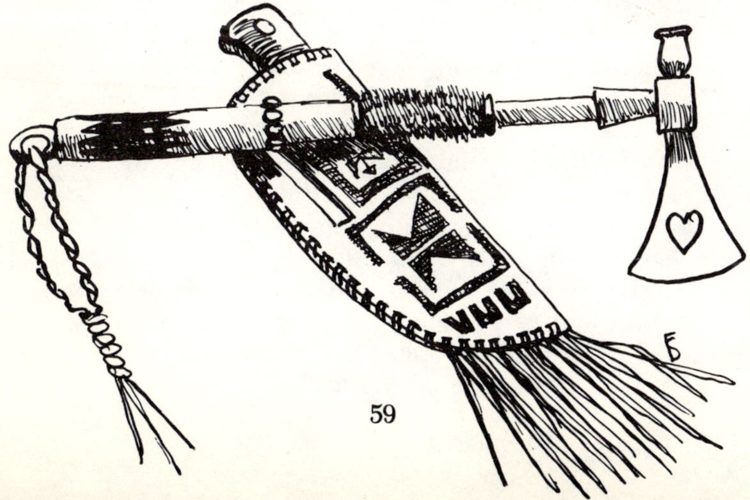

HORN CRAFT

Making your own powder horn or salt horn not only brings a lot of enjoyment, but also provides a great deal of satisfaction to the maker. The personal value also accelerates when it is handmade.

First, select a good basic horn. If you plan to engrave the horn, it should be light or white in the areas you plan to engrave. A horn with a black tip and a white body makes an excellent horn.

If the horn is raw, you need to boil the horn and clean out the membranes from the inside. You will also need to file or sand off the rough exterior down to the smooth horn. Sometimes you can buy horns from black-powder gun shops already cleaned and semipolished.

1. Saw off the open end until you have smooth even edges.
2. Cut off the tip of the horn and bore a small hole into the center cavity. It should only be large powder hole into the center cavity. It should only be large enough for the powder to flow freely from the horn—about the size of a matchstick.
3. Cut and carve a wooden plug for the large end of the horn. The plug should be about the size of the opening with a slight taper on the end. Be careful not to make it too small. The plug should have a ridge or overhang slightly larger than the opening.
4. Boil the horn until it is soft and pliable.
5. Drive the plug into the end of the horn while it is still soft.
6. Secure the plug into the horn near the top edge with nails or small pegs.
7. When the horn cools and hardens, it will conform and seal around the plug.
8. Grind or sand the plug to the desired shape.

9. Carve a small plug or stopper for the small end of the horn. It should be carved out of hardwood. Make the small end long enough to fit well into the horn. For variety and uniqueness, carve the stopper into the shape of an acorn, animal's head, bird's head, etc.

10. Some horn makers will carve or grind grooves, ridges, or other shapes on the small end of the horn. You will need at least one groove for your carrying strap.

11. Instead of sanding, some horn makers prefer to scrape down their horns with the edge of a piece of glass. This gives the horn a semifinish without polishing.

12. You may wish to scrape down your horn so it is thin enough to see how much powder you have when held up to a light. If so, this should be done before engraving the horn.

13. If you wish to engrave your horn, this is referred to as the "scrimshaw" procedure, with the following steps.

  A. Draw the design on your horn with a felt-tip pen. Old timers drew such things as animals, birds, Indian designs, ships, hunting scenes, or whatever suited their fancy. Use your imagination.

  B. Spray the design with hairspray or Fixit to keep it from smearing.

  C. With the point of a knife or other sharp instrument, etch or scratch the design well into the horn.

  D. Cover the design with black ink or thin paint.

E. Before the ink or paint has a chance to dry, wipe off all the surplus, leaving only the residue in the scratch marks. This will bring out your design in bold dark lines.

F. You may seal the design further with a coat of wax.

G. Polish the horn to the desired finish.

14. Make a leather shoulder strap for carrying the horn.

PLEASE NOTE:

A salt horn is made in much the same way as a powder horn, except it is much smaller.

HOW TO MAKE A POWDER HORN

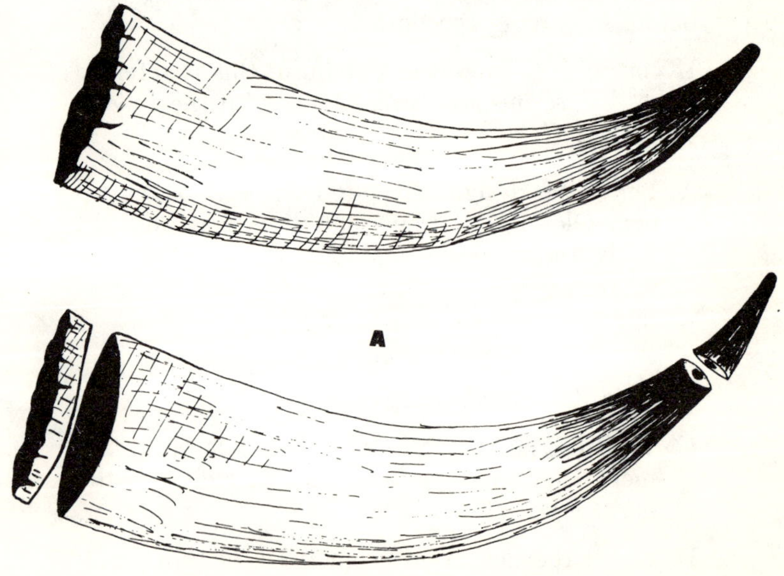

HORN CRAFT

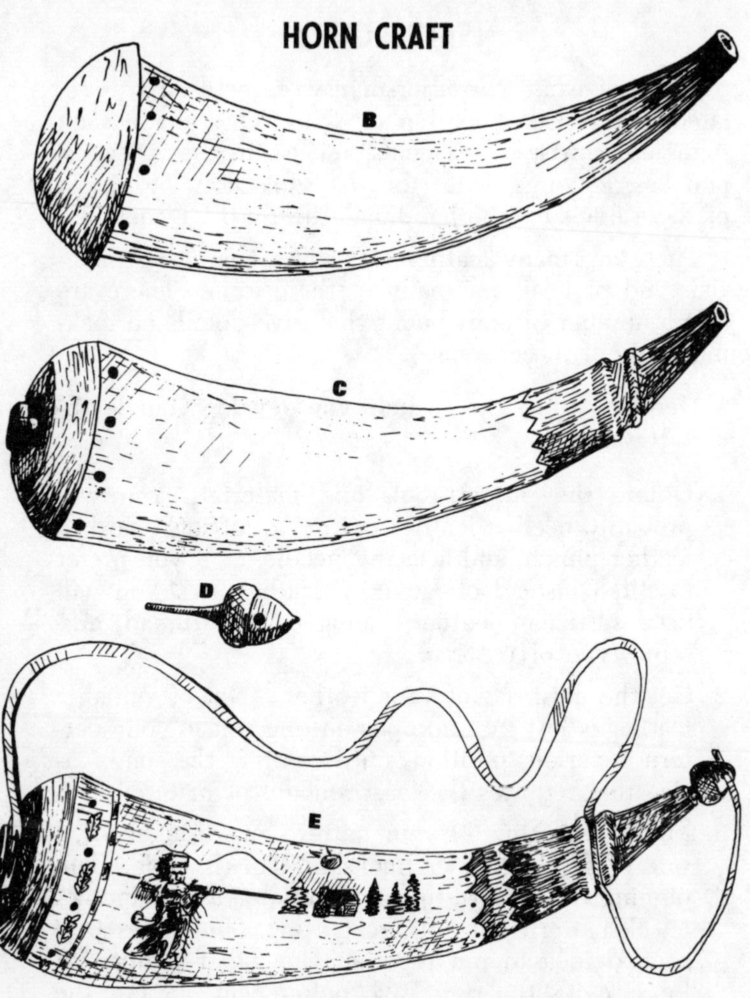

A. After cleaning and scraping horn, cut off both the large and little ends
   of the horn. Drill match size hole in small end of horn for powder
   spout.
B. Boil horn until soft then insert plug in large end—leaving about ¼
   inch overhand. Peg plug into horn.
C. Grind or file plug to desired shape. Also, carve small end including a
   strap groove.
D. Construct a powder stopper for small end of horn.
E. Engrave horn with desired design. Attach shoulder strap to horn.

LEATHERCRAFT

Much of what a frontiersman wore or used was related to the use of leather or skins. They made such items as: shirts, pants, coats, moccasins, belts, capes, pouches, leggings, knife sheaths, gun cases, etc. Most of these items can be handmade by the FCF member.

There are many leathercraft stores that have materials and patterns for many of these items. There are also a number of craft books that give details on making many of these items.

Here are a few tips to help you develop your leathercraft skills.

1. Obtain the proper tools and materials. You will probably need a leather cutter, a cutting board, a leather punch, and a lacing needle, or if you prefer to stitch instead of lacing, a leather awl. You will need sufficient leather, lacing or wax thread, and some type of pattern.

2. Get the most out of your leather. A lot of valuable leather is lost by improper cutting. Place your pattern in various positions until you find the combination that requires the least amount of material.

3. Mark the outline of your pattern on the unexposed side of the leather or buckskin. This is easier than pinning the pattern to the material. Always double-check pattern lines before cutting. Sometimes it is a good idea to pin together the paper pattern to be sure it's the right size before you cut out the leather.

4. It is much easier to get a neater job if you will temporarily glue seams together before you lace or stitch. However, be careful and do not allow any of the glue to show on the exposed surface. Glue

has a tendency to change the color of the leather.

5. Buckskin has a tendency to stretch. Keep this in mind when working with this material.

BEADWORK

Some frontiersmen decorated their clothing, pouches, moccasins, gun cases, and belts with Indian beadwork. This beadwork was not added to their work clothes, but to the clothing they wore on special occasions, such as rendezvous, etc.

If you wish to decorate some of your personal items, beaded strips and pieces of various shapes may be purchased from many Indian handcraft shops. However, many FCF members make their own beadwork. If you would like to give this a try, a number of handcraft shops have beads and other materials you will need to learn the art of beadwork.

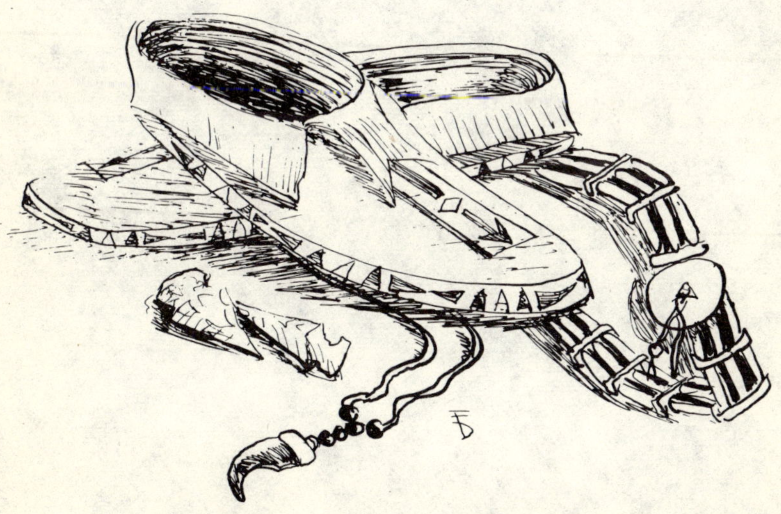

FRONTIER FOODS

When the early frontiersman went trapping or on a hunt, he traveled as light as possible, carrying only jerky, parched corn, or pemmican as food and foraging on natural food as he went.

The first lightweight camping or "traveling" food was jerky, then came the Indian pemmican. Both are as valuable and easy to make today as they were in the days of the frontiersman.

SMOKING MEAT

All types of meat including fish and fowl can be cured and smoked, enabling them to be used as a "traveling" food. By soaking them in a brine and then smoking them, meats will take on a hearty outdoor flavor.

Remember, when you smoke meats, it is only to preserve and add flavor to the meat. *You do not* cook meat in a smoker. The temperature inside the smoker should never exceed 150 degrees Fahrenheit and only "hard" woods are used to make smoke.

SIMPLE BRINE

This recipe for brine can be used for soaking *all* types of meat—it is very basic. Different flavorings can be added to suit the taste of the individual. Meat strips for jerky should be soaked for 10-12 hours!

Recipe for simple brine: 1 gallon water and 1 pound salt.

RECIPE FOR JERKY

Cut all fat from beef, then cut into thin slices. Soak in "simple brine" overnight. Hang meat in smoker and smoke from 4-6 hours. Remove from smoker and place in oven (200 degrees Fahrenheit) until meat is dry— about 2 hours.

HELFUL HINTS

Smoke birds at a temperature of 200-225 degrees Fahrenheit. When leg bone turns with ease in the socket it is done. Fish should be cleaned soon after they are caught. Remove slime with mixture of 1 part vinegar to 4 parts water. Rinse well. Cut off heads, leave tails on. Try not to puncture skin. Smoke at 80-85 degrees if fish is to be kept for a long period. In drying fish, a white liquid may ooze from the surface. This is not harmful or unpleasant. It is a tasty, nutritious, protein substance. Let it solidify on the surface of the fish.

PEMMICAN

Recipe for "Modern" Pemmican

Dried beef . . . . .8 oz.
Raisins . . . . .8 oz.
Unroasted peanuts or pecans . . . . .8 oz.
Honey . . . . .2 tsp.
Peanut butter . . . . .4 tbsp.
Cayenne pepper . . . . .¾ tsp.

1. Use jerky and dry it so meat will break and crumble.
2. Pound meat into powder or grind using an electric blender.
3. Add raisins, dried blueberries, chopped dried apricots, peaches, pecans, peanuts.
4. Heat honey and peanut butter to soften it, then blend into the mixture. Add the cayenne pepper and make sure it is worked thoroughly through the mixture.
5. If you want to go completely natural, pack the mixture into sausage casings or put it in plastic "tie bags."
6. Keep in a cool, dry place. Pemmican will keep indefinitely and can't be beat as a snack or lunch on the trail!

SMOKER

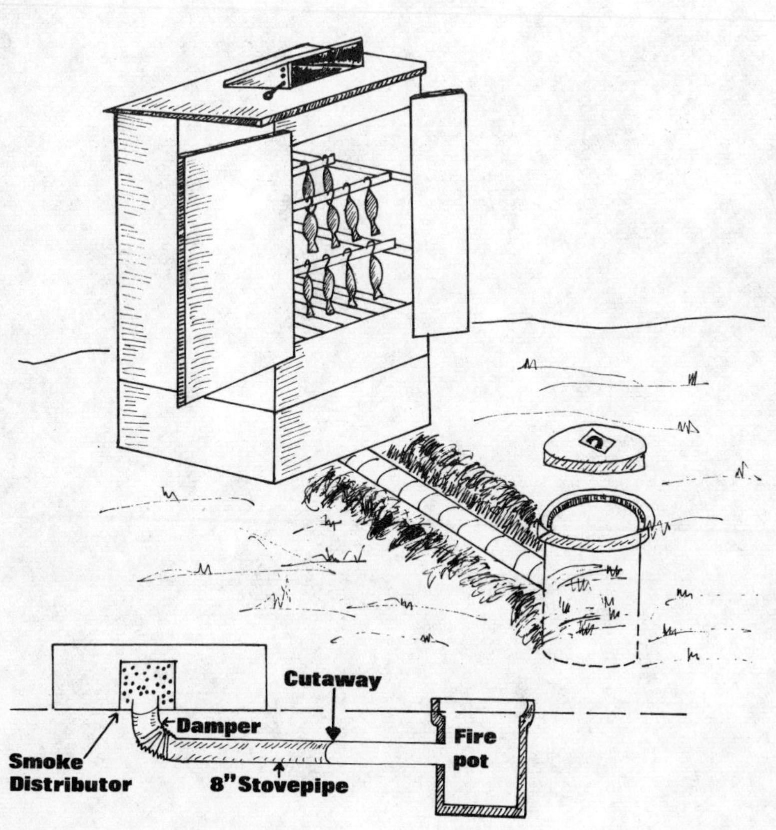

SHELTERS

If a frontiersman was in one place for a long period, he would no doubt build a log cabin. However, when on the move the frontiersman usually used the same type of portable shelter as the Indians, such as the tepee and the lodge.

Some historians believe the tepee of the Plains Indians was one of the most ideal shelters in existence. It was light in weight and easily and quickly erected.

By raising the slide flaps, it stayed cool in summer. With a fire in the center, it stayed warm in winter. By using a bull boat over the top of the smoke hole, it stayed dry during a rainstorm.

We encourage FCF members, if possible, to use a tepee for their shelter during FCF activities. It does have one disadvantage, it cannot be bug-proofed like many modern tents. However, its beauty, uniqueness, and historical nature far outweigh this disadvantage.

Tepees may be purchased from some tenting companies. There are a few places where you can purchase tepee poles. However, it is usually necessary to cut your own poles.

If you're fortunate enough to have a tepee, you'll find the novelty of sleeping and living in this shelter will really take you back in spirit to the days of the frontiersmen.

Primitive lean-to shelters and white wall tents were also used by the frontiersmen.

A. Tie 3 poles together into tripod.
B. Place 10 to 12 poles evenly around tripod leaving space for setting pole.
C. Tie tepee to setting pole and lift into place and arrange over poles.
D. Lace together in front, open smoke flap with poles. Smoke poles should be crossed in back. Stake down.

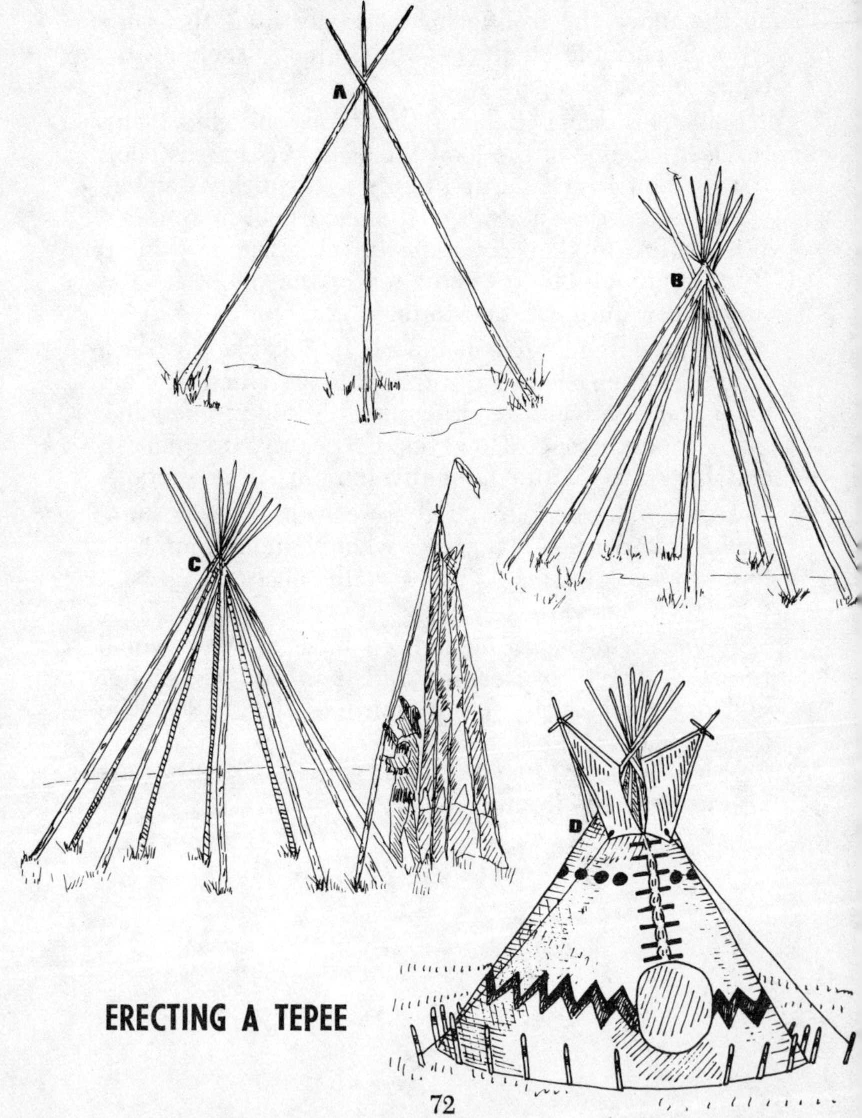

ERECTING A TEPEE

SPINNING A YARN

The ability of many old-timers to tell a story or relate an adventure was real art. They could keep listeners fascinated for hours. We encourage FCF members to develop the art of storytelling. If you develop the ability to use some of the terms unique to the frontiersmen, your story will have yet another dimension.

An example is the following story written by Fred Deaver, titled "A Heap of Trouble."

A HEAP OF TROUBLE
By Fred Deaver

Yes Siree, that's what I calls 'em. Black, brown, or ol' grizzly, they be bear and that means trouble. Yep, ya can't tell stories 'bout the frontier before someone will tell 'bout how they kill't a bear or how they almost got kill't by a bear.

Now ya see pilgrims, many years ago thar be bear everwhar ya would care to go in this great country of ours, and they was called many names. Now the Injuns sometimes called them Brother, the mountainman called him grizzly, silvertip, or ol' Ephraim, and many times pioneer and Injun alike called him names we just won't mention here.

One thing fer sure, the good Lord made quite a critter when he made ol' bear. Now the bear is a large fur-bearin' animal, and he be related to the dog. When a bear walks, he steps down on the entire sole of his foot as a man does. The bear has large, strong claws, and ol' bear can use them claws to rip a log open to git some honey, or he use 'em to dig up ants or to catch fish. They can break a moose's back with one swat of their powerful paws.

Now ya know ol' bear's got a short tail, and also get a short temper. Ol' grizz may look clumsy or slow, but pilgrim, bears have been known to run as fast as thirty miles an hour. I guess it be a good thing that bears hibernate; that is they eat a lot in the summer and fall, and sleep all winter.

Now most black bears usually weigh between two or three hundred pounds. Although they are called black, they may be brown, light brown, or cinnamon in color.

Now pilgrims, the grizzly bear be a shade from brown to blackish gray, and they got a big hump on their shoulders, and their hair be silvery gray. Now they may weigh as much as one thousand pounds and be ten feet tall.

I reckon the biggest bear be the brown bear, better known as the Kodiak bear. He may weigh as much as fifteen hundred pounds and be eleven feet tall.

Well now pilgrim, I reckon ya see now why that ol' bear can be a heap o' trouble when he wants to.

Well sir, the Injuns and pioneers had a great respect for the bear. The Injuns used to count it a great honor to count "coupe," that is, to touch a live bear and not kill it—or get kill't doing it. They knowed twer bad medicine to mess around with ol' bear. Now pilgrim, I'll tell ya a story that goes like this.

'Bout 1828 or 1830, when they was good fur trade and beaver skin were same as gold in yar poke, ol' Joe Meek, a mighty mountainman and free trapper, were at one of the big rendezvous—up in Yallarstone country it be. Now ol' Joe thought himself to be a mighty brave man, and were a mind to say so.

Now it seems that Joe's bravery weren't as much as another trapper thought his were. So Joe and this here other trapper got into it over which one were the bravest. It looked like thar were gonna be a shoot-out to settle the matter, when 'bout that time an ol' grizzly bear came walkin' into camp. Now pilgrim, ol' Joe run right up that ol' grizz, and whipped out his shootin' stick and slapped the grizz three times across his nose before he shot'em with his big bore (Hawkins rifle). And that ended the fussin' over who be the bravest.

Well sir, I know you've heard 'bout ol' Daniel Boone and Davey Crockett, and how they'd brag 'bout how they could "grin" a bear to death. Well now, that be truer than ya might think, pilgrim. Cause ye see, back in them days, what with the ol' flintlock shootin' irons they had, ya only had one shot, and if 'un ya just wounded or ya missed, they weren't nothin' else left to do 'cept jest stand thar and grin!

Well now, pilgrim, ya take ol' Lewis and Clark. When they went up into the Yallarstone, they told 'bout how hard twer to put ol' Ephraim to ground, with the wepuns they carried. Seems that ol' grizz could carry more lead in his hide than a good mountain man could carry in his huntin' pouch. So it was that they stayed clear of ol' "heap-o-trouble" when they could.

Well now, pilgrim, even today ol' bear is still respected—an' even feared. Many a modern-day sportsman consider the grizzly bear more dangerous than the African lion, and it might surprise ya to know that each year folks still get mauled and kill't in this country by bear.

Well now back in the early 1800's they were a famous mountainman name of Jedidiah Smith. Ol' Jed were a leadin' some trappers up the west side o' Black Hills when all a suddenly ol' Jed were face to face with ol' grizz, and fore they could drive the bear off, ol' Jed lay gashed and bleedin', with some ribs broke. Seems the bear had got ol' Jed's head in his jaws and near scalped him. With one ear almost tore off, ol' Jed told a feller the name of Clyman to get a needle and thread

an get to sewin'. Well sir, ol' Clyman did a right nice job stitchin' and in ten days ol' Jed were up and leadin' his trappers on into Crow Injun country.

Well now, pilgrim, let me tell ya one better'n that'en 'bout Jed.

Seems they were a Major Andrew Henry, leadin' some thirteen trappers fer a man name of General Ashley, head of a big fur company. I reckon it were in the spring of 1823, when 'bout one hundred miles out of Fort Kiowa a man name ol' Hugh Glass with Major Henry's party was out ahead of the rest of the trappers. When all a suddenly ol' sow grizzly with two cubs charged ol' Hugh Glass. Now ol' Glass took aim an' shot that ol' grizz sow right in the chest. But twern't enough to kill that ol' sow, and she caught Hugh after a short chase.

Now ol' Hugh whipped out his butcher knife and did all he could to defend hisself, but the bear near kill't ol' Hugh. It looked like Hugh were a gone beaver. Everone figgered he wouldn't last that night, but come sunup ol' Hugh were still hangin' on. So Major Henry asked fer a couple of men to stay till ol' Hugh give up the ghost. Right off a young man whose name would become famous in due time volunteered to stay. His name were Jim Bridger. Now another man, who were somewhat reluctant to do it, said he'd stay. His name were John Fitzgerald. Major Henry reckoned he'd pay $40 each fer riskin' losin' their scalps to stay with ol' Hugh.

Now ol' Hugh still were hangin' on, and each day it looked like his last. Now this went on fer five days, and ol' Fitzgerald said he'd stayed as long as he were gonna. If 'un Jim wanted to keep his hair he'd best come with him and leave Hugh. He was same as dead anyway. So it was that Jim Bridger and John Fitzgerald left Hugh Glass to die—alone. Now they took Hugh's rifle, knife, and all his fix-uns.

Well now I tell ya pilgrims, ol' Hugh's life didn't look worth a British musket ball. But ol' Hugh didn't give up. He ate berries and drank water from a nearby spring. Now Hugh were in much pain and couldn't walk, but all Hugh could think 'bout were getting even with Jim and John for leavin' him to die. Now ol' Hugh were able to kill a rattler fer meat, and each day Hugh got stronger.

One day he saw some wolves that had jest kill't a buffalo calf. Now Hugh crawled up close to that kill and fer the first time since he had been mauled by the bear, Hugh with all his strength stood on his feet and ran the wolves off with a club. And so the story went. Ol' Hugh survived seven weeks after the bear attack, and crawled and walked a hundred and fifty miles through hostile territory back to Fort Kiowa.

Well now, when ol' Hugh finally found Jim, you can imagine how Jim must of felt. But ol' Hugh forgive Jim Bridger and John Fitzgerald after all, and so be it.

Well pilgrim, ya can see why Injuns and frontiersmen wore their bear-claw necklaces with pride, and a bearskin robe is mighty nice on a cold winter night. And bear meat ain't too bad if 'un that's all ya got— after all meat's meat.

But I tell ya all, this ol' child is gonna always give old silvertip, Ephraim, and grizz the right-of-way on any trail we happen to meet! Cause ya see ol' Hawkeye aims to keep his skin in one piece, and most of all stay out of a heap o' trouble.

ORGANIZATION STRUCTURE

DISTRICT CHAPTERS

The basic unit of FCF is a district chapter. Each chapter elects its own officers with the exception of chairman. In this case, the district commander becomes chairman by virtue of his office. Chapter officers are: president, vice-president, and scribe. A district scout and assistant scout are also elected from among the boys to serve on the chapter staff.

CHAPTER NAME

To further emphasize the traditions of the Frontiersmen Camping Fraternity, each district chapter selects a historical name. This could be the name of a famous frontiersman in the area, an indian tribe, a historical site, or geographical location that played an important role in the state's history. For example, the chapter in the Southern Missouri District is the "Daniel Boone Chapter."

Become familiar with your chapter name by doing research on the subject. Develop a sense of pride in being a member of your chapter.

CHAPTER TRACE

The chapter plans at least one special event for FCF members during the year, usually some type of rugged outdoor adventure. This is also usually the time for the chapter's annual business session.

REGIONS

The Royal Rangers program is divided into eight
geographical regions. Each region is supervised by a
regional coordinator. The regional coordinator is also
the regional FCF officer. Some regions also have special events for FCF members, such as the "Regional
Pow AMU" in the South Central Region.

TERRITORIES

To further assist in the promotion and development
of FCF, the United States is divided into four territories—Mountainmen (West), Plainsmen (Midwest),
Riflemen (South), and Colonial (East). An FCF territorial representative is appointed by the national Royal
Rangers commander to serve each of these territories.
These representatives become national vice-presidents
of FCF by virtue of their office. A territorial scout and
an assistant territorial scout are elected to represent the Royal-Rangers-age boys in each territory.

TERRITORIAL RENDEZVOUS

Each territory has a rendezvous every 2 years. A
rendezvous is an outdoor event that includes such
events as a black-powder shoot, tomahawk throwing,
knife throwing, best costume, flint and steel, trading,
and other frontier-related activities.

FCF TERRITORIES AND CHAPTERS

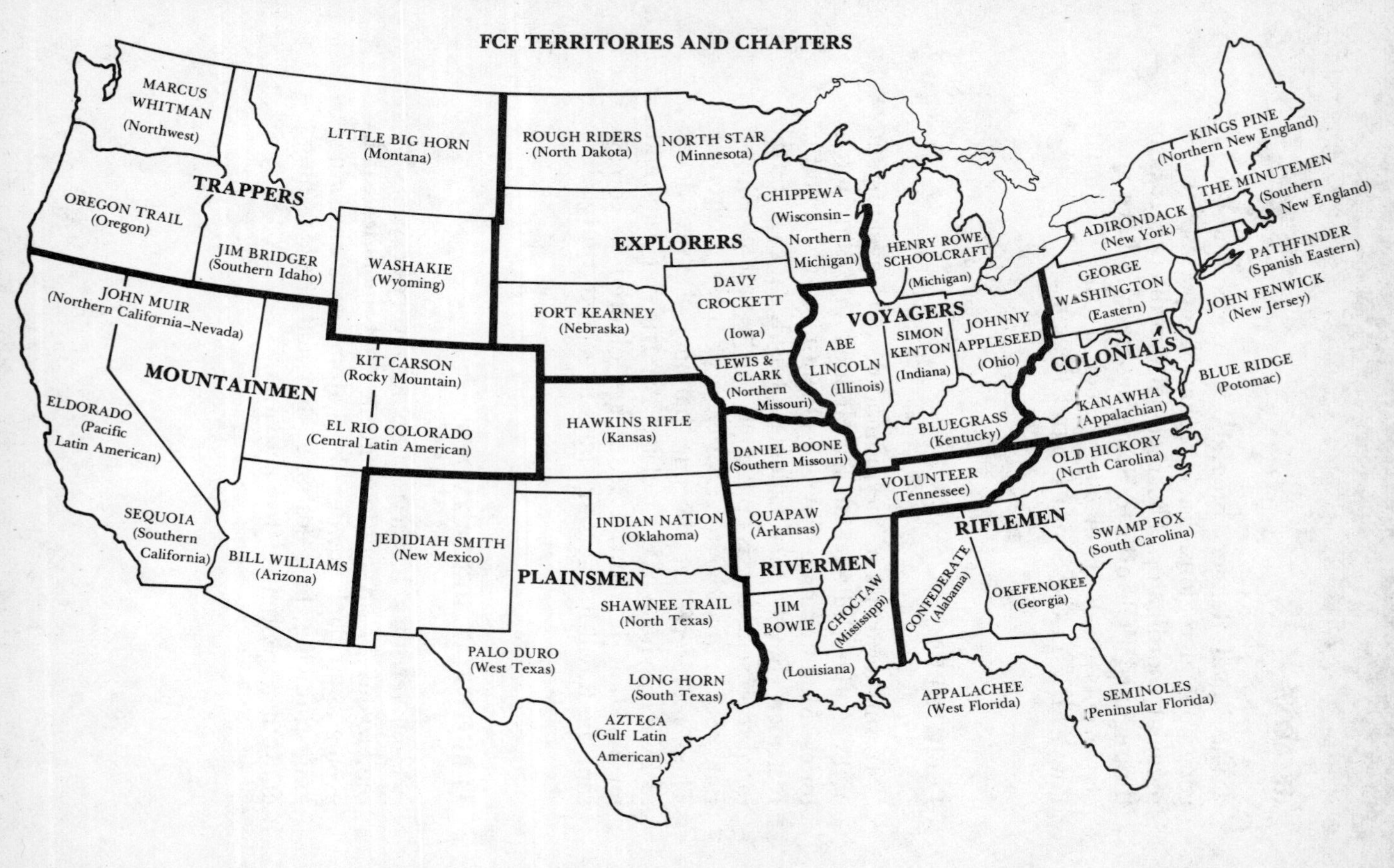

NATIONAL

To give national recognition to the program and to further assist in its development, a national FCF president is elected. A national scout and an assistant national scout are also elected to represent the boys in the total FCF program. The national president is elected at the national rendezvous and the national scout and assistant national scout are elected at the national rendezvous or the national camporama. Their term of office is 2 years. The president's term of office is 4 years. A national scribe and a national historian are appointed by the national president.

A national rendezvous is conducted every 4 years. This outstanding event not only includes a black-powder shoot, tomahawk throwing, knife throwing, best costume, flint and steel, and trading, but also a number of colorful ceremonies, pageants, special features, unusual services, and outstanding speakers.

OLD-TIME RENDEZVOUS

During the 1800's, the beaver hat was in great demand. This placed a great demand on beaver pelts, which were used to make the hats. To meet this demand, the mountains in the West were soon infested by a special breed of frontiersmen that became known as "mountainmen."

These fur trappers soon adopted many of the ways of the Indians. These men adapted to the life of the mountains and the wilderness so well, most were reluctant to leave and travel back to civilization. The only problem was the mountainmen needed a market for their furs and they also needed to replenish their supplies such as salt, powder, and shot, and from time to time to replace certain equipment like traps, pots, knives, axes, and rifles.

To meet this need of the mountainmen, certain traders from back east would travel west into the mountains to a predetermined location or rendezvous. They would trade the mountainmen the supplies they needed in return for their furs. Most mountainmen took most of the price of their furs in trading goods because they had little need for money. Thus, the famous rendezvous was born.

The site was usually in a valley where there was a good stream and plenty of grass for grazing. The traders would arrive first with their wagons and packhorses laden with trade goods.

Soon from out of the mountains all over the West the mountainmen came. Clad in their best buckskins, they approached the rendezvous at a full gallop, whooping and shouting and firing their guns in the air. There was even more shouting when they spied an old friend.

The Indian wives of many of the mountainmen soon had the valley dotted with colorful tepees. Many friendly Indians also attended, adding to the color.

Most of these mountainmen lived a rather isolated life much of the year, so they were determined to make this the one big event of the year.

Many were eager to demonstrate their improved skills, so there were contests of various kinds from horse racing to black-powder shooting.

Huge pots of cooking food were soon emptied, and far into the night, laughter, shouting, and singing echoed throughout the valley. They shared new adventures or retold old ones, or perhaps gave a tribute to a friend who didn't live to make it to that rendezvous.

Notable mountainmen such as Jim Bridger, Jed Smith, John Colter, Kit Carson, Jim Meeker, Hugh Glass, and Jeremiah Johnson attended these rendezvous.

These events sometimes attracted individuals other than traders, Indians, and mountainmen. Famous frontier preachers, artists, and historians were among those who attended, each giving their version of the event.

All too soon, the mountainmen rode back into the mountains with hopes of returning to next year's rendezvous.

Most historians agree that these rendezvous were the most colorful events ever held in the west. When the beaver trade died and the last rendezvous was held, a great frontier tradition vanished. However, today's frontiersmen in FCF are reviving this tradition in the territorial and national rendezvous.

THE FCF SONG

words and music by John Eller

FRED DEAVER
'84

Frontiersmen Pledge

"I share with you the warmth and glow of this campfire. These crimson flames are a symbol of the fellowship and an adventure in camping. They also remind me that I should endeavor at all times to share with you the warmth of Christian friendship, and to share with others the light of my Christian testimony. I also promise to do my best to keep alive the spirit of F.C.F. in my personal life and to observe at all times the principles of the Royal Rangers program."

TRAPPERS BRIGADE

The Trappers Brigade is a special auxiliary group within the Frontiersmen Camping Fraternity. It was established during the 1978 National Council for the purpose of promoting additional Christian service among F.C.F. members.

Three basic steps of recognition have been established. They are the Company Trapper, the Bourgeois (pronounced Boohz-wah'), and the Free Trapper. Trapper Brigade points will be given in varying amounts for various types of Christian service. The number of points required for the Company Trapper will be twenty. The Bourgeois requires 40 additional points and the Free Trapper needs 60 points above the number required for Bourgeois. Each additional 30 points earned will entitle the Free Trapper to receive a numeral to be placed on his trapper's medal. All active members are eligible to work towards Trappers Brigade recognition regardless of whether or not they have attained Buckskin or Wilderness status.

To get credit points toward Trappers Brigade recognition, the projects may meet one or more of the following criteria:

(1) Projects may represent a desperate need (possibly a crisis) on the part of a church or individual that would have exceptional difficulty meeting that need.

(2) The project should be over and above organized church activity in which the person would be expected to participate as a member of the church.

(3) A log of activity must be maintained on the back of the person's F.C.F. membership

card* and approved by the person's pastor and certified by a District F.C.F. officer.

Note: Work for a relative which would normally be done otherwise would not count for Trappers Brigade points. Also, we do not want to have a person's spiritual life, Royal Ranger Ministry, church work, job, or family life suffer as a result of effort towards Trapper Brigade Recognition.

Types of Christian Service Projects

Basically, group projects would be such as:

(1) Rebuilding a church for some small community in case of disaster.

(2) Repairing or rebuilding a home for the aged or needy families.

(3) Working on fundraising projects that would help buy the necessities of life for the needy people of the community or missionaries.

(4) Procuring, preparing, and delivering food baskets to needy families, etc., would also be considered.

Note: Only with special approval and in unusual circumstances would points be given for cash contributions to a needy cause. The work on a fund-raising project, however, would be considered an act of Christian service.

Point System

Since the F.C.F. and the Royal Rangers is a boys' ministry, there is a built-in emphasis on boy participation in the Trappers Brigade. Boys will earn one credit point per hour of work. Men will earn one credit point when they are responsible for a boy being involved in the same project; otherwise they

---

(*) It would be a good idea to also keep a record in the back of your F.C.F. handbook in case you lose one of your past membership cards.

earn ½ point per hour. Travel time is not considered as work time for credit.

Frontiersmen working toward Trappers Brigade must be members in good standing. As examples, (1) current and previous years dues must be paid, (2) they must have participated in at least one-half of the District F.C.F. activities in the previous and current year, and (3) they must be active in the Royal Rangers and in their church.

Through the Trappers Brigade Christian Service Projects, the Frontiersmen Camping Fraternity takes on a new image. Remember, the F.C.F. is usually judged by the image we have, the impression we leave, and the reputation we build for the organization.

TRAPPERS BRIGADE PINS
(To be worn behind F.C.F. Membership Pin)

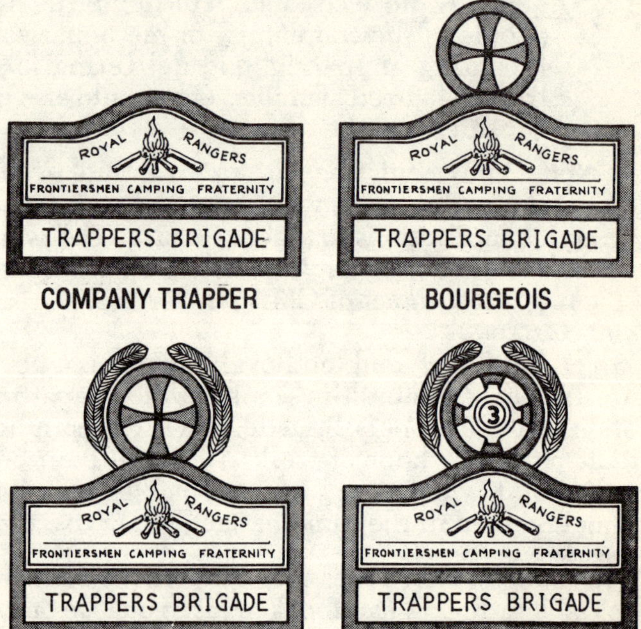

COMPANY TRAPPER

BOURGEOIS

FREE TRAPPER

FREE TRAPPER
3rd Time Pin

FRED DEAVER
1984

NOTES AND PERSONAL RECORDS

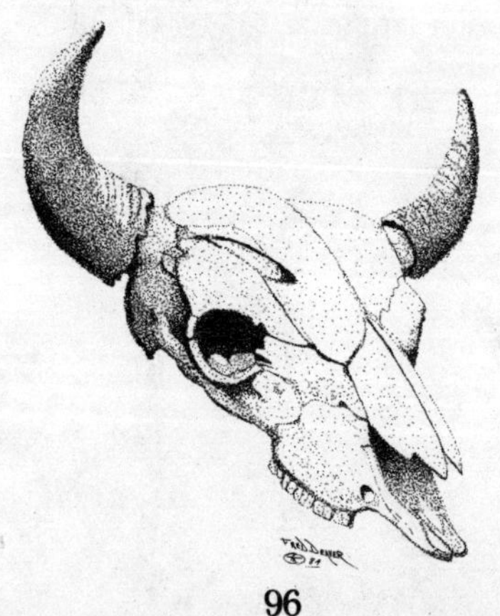